THE ORIGINAL IRISH RECIPE BOOK

Compiled and edited by Viola Dono

Analogy Press
Belfast

The Original Irish Recipe Book

First published in the UK & Ireland in 2015 by Analogy Press, Belfast

ISBN 9780993095900

British Library Cataloguing in Publication Data
A CIP catalogue record for this book is available from the British Library

Published by Analogy Press, Belfast

Contents

Bill of Fare - Numerical Index 5

Growing up in an Irish kitchen 13

Dinners 17

Irish Portraits 55

Sweet Bakes 73

Desserts & Puddings 89

Traybakes- Irish Favourites 111

Irish Soft Drinks 125

Irish Cocktails & Liqueurs 131

Irish Jams 143

The Irish Bakeboard 151

Handy Tables 182

American Cup Conversions 184

Glossary 186

Ingredient Equivalents 190

Acknowledgements 192

Alphabetical Index 195

Menu Suggestions 204

Front cover artwork reproduced from 'Still Life with Raisin Cake, Fruit and Wine' by William Michael Harnett born 10th August, 1848 in Clonakilty, County Cork, Ireland, died 29th October, 1892, New York, U.S.A

Bill Of Fare

(alphabetical page index at back of book)

IRISH DINNERS

1. Freshly caught Irish trout grilled over an open fire
2. An Irish Mixed Grill
3. Pancakes Colleen
4. Easy, Tasty Irish Stew
5. Brown Stew
6. Irish Stout Stew
7. Creamy Irish Colcannon Mash
8. Salmon Frumenty
9. Lamb Dinner by the Peat Turf Fire
10. Fillet Steak in a Bramble Jus
11. Scrambled Eggs with Irish Smoked Salmon
12. Irish Salmon Fish Cakes
13. Vegetable Marrow Bake
14. Wild Atlantic Seafood Crumble
15. Cú Chulainn Salmon
15b. Emer's Sauce 15c. Lobster Sauce
16. Skellig Islands Trout
17. Fillet of Sole with Irish Dulse Seaweed
18. Atlantic Coast Seafood Tian
19. Dublin Bay Prawn Cocktail
20. Dublin Rarebit
21. Traditional Dublin Bacon Coddle
22. Stuffed Sausages
23. Lough Erne Eel Pie
24. Harvey's Sauce
25. Donegal Pie Recipe
26. Donegal Crab Quiche
27. Lobster Cream
28. Fish Mould
28b. Boiled Mayonnaise Sauce
29. Leitrim Brawn Recipe
30. Craiceann
31. Old Dublin Seafood Salad
32. Anraith an Lae - Soup of the Day
33. Irish Nettle & Oatmeal Broth

34. Vine Tomatoes stuffed with Irish Smoked Salmon
35. Belfast Chip Shop Pastie Recipe
36. Homemade Sausage Rolls
37. Belfast Batch Bread Snacks
38. Prátaí Inis Ceithleann
39. Atlantic Herring Log
40. Meatloaf
41. Old-fashioned Stuffing Recipe
42. Irish Hotch Potch
43. Poached Cod Roes
44. Old Belfast recipe for Chicken Omelette
45. Smoked Haddock & Cheese Savoury
46. Promisques (an old breakfast dish)
47. Eggs Prince Congal
48. Gaelic Steak
49. Fillet of Beef
50. Galantine of Rabbit
51. Little Pheasant Creams
52. Creamy Cider Trout
53. Fish Steamed Between Two Plates
54. Tomato Sauce
55. Marrow Dumplings for Soups & Broths
56. Nettle Stuffing
57. Cabbage in Butter
58. Baked Limerick Ham in Cider
59. Goat Kid Meat Stew
60. Cottage Potatoes
61. Pan Seared Breast of Pheasant
62. Scallion Champ
63. Lentil Irish Stew
64. Ragout of Mutton
65. Dun Laoghaire Fried Plaice
66. Minted Peas
67. Parsley Butter
68. Ham Butter
69. Grilled Lamb Chops with Victoria Plums
70. Sunday Roast Salmon
71. West Coast Smoked Salmon Surprise
72. Devilled Crab
73. Stewed Stuffed Shoulder of Irish Rosé Veal
74. Veal Stuffing

IRISH PORTRAITS

75. Cherry Cakes
76. Marrow Marmalade
77. Wheaten Fadge
78. An Apple Hedgehog
79. Tory Island Cabbage
80. St. Patrick's Pudding
81. Gracie McDermott's Salmon Bisque
82. Gracie's Salad Dressing
83. Vinegar Pastry
84. Spiced Beef
85. Brown Sauce
86. Rhubarb or Gooseberry Chutney
87. Parsley Honey
88. Turnip au Gratin
89. Rissoles
90. Urney Pudding
91. Ginger Wine
92. Baked Salmon Trout
93. Buttermilk Brack
94. Ivory Cream Recipe
95. Brown Soda Bread
96. Potato Pastry
97. Tuesday's Pudding / Steamed Scrap Bread Pudding
98. Sherry
99. Sponge Cake

IRISH BAKING

100. Belfast Florence Cake
101. Date 'n' Walnut Cake
102. Kerry Apple Cake
103. Irish Porter Cake
104. Simple Irish Baker's Short Paste
105. Blackcurrant & Bramley Apple Tart
106. Irish Plate Apple Tart (really thin pastry)
107. Apple Tart (thick pastry)
108. Irish Boiled Fruit Cake
109. Pineapple Boiled Fruit Cake

110. Gluten Free Yogurt Cake
111. Rose Fondant Icing
112. Chocolate Cake
112b. Chocolate Icing
113. Seed Cake with Almonds
114. Bramley Apple Gingerbread
115. Botanic Apple Cheesecakes
116. Coconut Macaroon Tartlets
117. Pineapple Creams
118. Irish Rock Buns
119. Mum's easy 3,4,5,6 Buns
120. Chocolate Faery Cakes
121. Little Honey Cakes
122. Erin Cakes

IRISH PUDDINGS

123. Orange & Blackberry Pudding
124. Irish Honeycomb Cheesecake
124b. Homemade Honeycomb Recipe
125. Mint Choc Bubble Bar Cheesecake
126. Almond Rice Cream
127. Irish Bramley Apple Meringue Pudding
128. Irish Apple Sponge Pudding
129. Semolina Pudding
130. Baked Tapioca & Apple Pudding
131. Bramley Apple Fool
132. Steamed Rhubarb
133. Next Day Blackberries
134. Bramble Duff Pudding
135. Blackberry & Bramley Apple Autumn Pudding
136. Wild Blackberry Dessert Jelly
137. Early 20th century old Blackberry Roll recipe
138. Stewed Blackberries and Apple
139. Hot Apple & Blackberry Trifle
140. Wild Blackberry Topping (for yogurt or cheesecake)
141. Irish Bread & Butter Pudding
142. Almond Topped Gooseberry Pie
143. Sticky Toffee Sauce
144. Border of Rice with Plums
145. Fruit Compote
146. Rhubarb Crumble
147. Bramloffee Pie

148. Potato Apple
149. Potato Pudding
150. Cheat's Irish Christmas Plum Pudding in a Flash
151. Christmas Pudding
152. Brandy Butter
153. Christmas Crumble
154. Buttermilk Dumpling
155. Jam Sauce for Plain Sponge Puddings
156. Hot Whiskey Sauce for Puddings
157. Semolina Jelly
158. Sago Pudding with Bramble Jelly
159. Redcurrant Bread & Butter Pudding
160. Irish Coffee Dessert Cake
161. Irish Coffee Jelly

IRISH TRAYBAKES

162. Pineapple Delights
163. Mum's Fruit Squares
164. Oaten Apple Slice
165. Paradise Squares
166. Marshmallow Crispy Squares
167. Fifteens
168. Almond Slices
169. Marie's Bars
170. Ginger Sponge Squares
171. Bride's Slices
172. Mallow Snowballs
173. Lemon Coconut Slices
174. Biscuit Fudge
175. Chocolate Peppermint Squares
176. Oaten Shortbread
177. Celtic Tiger Shortbread
178. Chapel Windows
179. Granny's Favourite Traybake
180. Date Slices
181. Gur or Chester Cake
182. Red Currant Fudge

IRISH DRINKS, SOFT

183. Almond or Hazelnut Milk
184. Strawberry Crush
185. Bramble Cordial
186. Blackberry Shake
187. Oatmeal Gruel
188. Barley Water
189. Blackcurrant Tea
190. Rose Syrup
191. Irish Moss (Carrageen) Lemonade
192. Apple Water
193. Donegal Carrageen Moss Drink
194. Irish Raspberry Syrup
195. Dandelion Punch
196. Elderflower Cordial
197. Non -Alcoholic Irish Coffee
198. Irish Berry Smoothie

IRISH COCKTAILS AND LIQUEURS

199. Sligo Slop
200. Ratafia
201. Vintage Irish Cider Fruit Cup Recipe
202. Emerald Isle
203. The Irish Blackthorn
204. Everybody's Irish
205. Irish Almond Cocktail
206. Irish Fix
207. The Blarney Stone
208. Irish Shillelagh
209. The Tipperary Cocktail
210. Irish Cooler
211. Kerry Cooler
212. Cold Irish Coffee
213. Retro 20th Century Hot Irish Coffee
214. Irish Tea
215. Misty Irish Cocktail
216. Mulled Beer
217. Hot Buttered Irish
218. Hot Irish Whiskey & Port Drink
219. Irish Alexander on the Rocks
220. Whiskey Honey

221. Irish Shamrock
222. Irish lemonade
223. Irish Cider Cup
224. Irish Apple Bowl
225. Mc Brandy

IRISH JAMS

226. Apple Clove Jam
227. Strawberry & Gooseberry Jam
228. Plum & Apple Jam
229. Raspberry & Redcurrant Jam
230. Damson Jam
231. Rhubarb Jam
232. Rhubarb & Ginger Jam
233. Rowan & Apple Jam (a 1944 recipe)
234. Irish Blackcurrant Jam
235. Sloe & Apple Jelly
236. Lemon Cheese for Tarts
237. Microwave Lemon & Rose Curd
238. Blackberry Curd
239. Rose Petal Jelly
240. Green Gooseberry Jelly
241. Mint Jelly

IRISH BREADS

242. Easy Oat Bread
243. Silver Grove Brown Soda Bread
244. Irish Potato Bread with Bacon
245. Old Dublin Pancakes Recipe
246. Soft Irish Brown Soda Bread / Wheaten Bread
247. Grandmother's Pancakes
248. Indian Meal Griddle Pancakes Recipe
249. Potato Pancake
250. Boxty Pancakes
251. Springhill Sultana Scones
252. Yogurt Scones
253. County Tyrone Wheaten Scones
254. Glencar Faery Scones
255. Griddle Scones

256. Breadcrumb Griddle Scones
257. Fluffy Light Potato Scones
258. Coconut Scones
259. Rhubarb & Custard Scones
260. Goat's Milk Wheaten Scones
261. Irish Restaurant Rich Wheaten Bread
262. Praitie Oaten / Reusel / Potato Oaten Recipe
263. Irish Treacle Bread
264. Treacle Fadge Farls
265. Buttermilk Oaten Bread
266. Granny's Lightly Spiced Fruit Soda Bread
267. Sultana Bran Soda Bread
268. Malt Soda Bread
269. Fadge Bread
270. Paddy's Pizzas with a Fadge / Soda Farl Base
271. Lamb & Mint Paddy's Pizza
272. Ulster Fry Paddy's Pizza
273. Irish Garden Paddy's Pizza
274. Buttermilk Point Picnic Loaf
275. Extra Rich Fruit Loaf
276. Moist Irish Teabread
277. Mrs Mulligan's Whiskey Tea Bread
278. Fast Food Savoury Pie Pastry
279. Stampy Bread – a type of Boxty
280. Chewy Malt Raisin Bread
281. Bramley Apple Scones
282. Irish Stout Bread
283. Tomato Bread
284. Cheddar Bread
285. Yogurt & Banana Bread
286. Shelled Hemp Soda Bread
287. Savoury Pancakes
288. Spelt Bread
289. Scones Made With Cream
290. Boiled Milk Scones
291. Cheese Muffins
292. Sophia's Soda Bread
293. Hot Cross Buns
294. Bramley Apple Brack
295. Donkey Lugs

Growing up in an Irish kitchen...

I was born in Enniskillen, Northern Ireland in 1968. My life's journey with food began with a seemingly endless supply of home-grown fresh fruit and vegetables. Throughout my childhood Mum and Dad kept two fields of land hand-planted out with beetroot, broccoli, cabbages, cauliflower, lettuce, leeks, onions, scallions, potatoes, vegetable marrows, soup celery, parsley, straw-berries, raspberries, redcurrants, blackcurrants, gooeseberries, and sweet pea flowers, for sale to restaurants and homes in the surrounding towns and villages. Many customers would drive for miles to buy food straight from the fields, and often shared their best recipes with my Mum Betty. Mum would hurriedly scribble these down on little pieces of paper and bundle them into the dresser drawer before rushing back out to tend to her market garden.

I wrote my first book in 2011, after 20 years running a wholesale bakery supplying hundreds of retail outlets across the United Kingdom and Ireland. It was a handbook of commercial bakers' recipes, written in the quantities and measurements for industrial size mixers. My second book stepped back in time, delving into old books and records from my Grandparents' and Great-Grandparents' days. It was called 'Dreams & Recipes 1904 - 1914' and won me 'Food Writer of the Year' for Northern Ireland in 2014. It was inevitable then that my third book should be a transferring of all those market garden archives, on all those little pieces of paper, carefully stashed away in the dresser drawer. It had suddenly dawned on me, the irreplacable nature of the recipes in my family's custody, and how important it was that they shouldn't just disappear. The recipes came from all sorts of people, from all parts of Northern Ireland and the Republic, and are presented here amongst my own family recipes, pretty much in their original form. As the book began to take form other recipes were generously offered, many of which were so interesting I included them in the chapter 'An Irish Portrait'. I chose to call the book *The Original Irish Recipe Book* because the recipes are orignal Irish ones, in the original form in which I found them, just as they were originally made in Irish homes. I have transcribed the recipes into twenty-first century English, only where a better understanding of the process or equipment was needed. There are all sorts of recipes – from breads baked in traditional Irish bakeries, to Irish lunchtime snacks, dinners and cake, right through to contemporary Irish drinks recipes served in the best cocktail lounges around the world.

The great beauty of Irish recipes is that most rarely call for any fancy kitchen equipment at all. Ovens were not high spec and most Irish recipes could be made on the most basic of ovens or firesides. In Great-Grandmother's day, practically every day was baking day, with pancakes and breads in daily demand. The bake-board was seldom idle. Tools were very simple - the bake-board was for kneading, there was a glazed yellow bowl for mixing, and a crock full of buttermilk with a dipping tin. Most Irish kitchens had a flat yellow handled knife, which was perfect for mixing the bread dough and for scraping the bake-board. A goose wing was kept for sweeping the board and griddle free of excess flour. A potato ricer, or for those who couldn't afford it, a wooden pounder called a beetle was used to turn mashed potatoes into soft vermicelli-like strands. The most amazing array of wonderful breads was produced from these primitive baking tools.

The recipes are as wide ranging and diverse as the local accents and dialects you will hear should you travel all the way from Cushendall to the Bay of Clonakilty. A vintage recipe for Leitrim Brawn may seem unusual today, but just over a century ago Brawn graced R.M.S. Titanic's buffet menu on April 14, 1912. Fare such as Paddy's Pizzas and Bramley Apple Toffee Pie are more likely to appear on a buffet table these days. The traybake recipes were included by request of friends and family abroad, who always make straight for the freshly filled traybake tins as they walk through the door on visits home.

I hope that the wide range of recipes in this book portray a little of our forty shades of green, and all the other colours that intermingle to make this little island what it is today. I hope too that you will prove true my Granda's belief, that you can make as good or better at home than you will find in any *aytin' house* (the waggish Hiberno-English term for restaurant) in the world.

So come with me and we'll peek through some Irish kitchen windows, and together share a taste of a little island which nestles at the far western edge of Europe; an island which I'm so very proud to call home.

Irish Dinners

Robbing the plover's nest for her small eggs, and the
wild bee's hoard for his honey,
And netting the fat gold-spangled trout from the
frosty mountain stream,
With China tea and white farls we buy for the smallest silver money,
We shall eat and dream.

And wait in the Irish twilight for the high moon that is
late in coming,
And nothing shall break in to unquiet the deep warm peace,
But the call of a distant eagle, or the bittern's drumming,
Or the shrill wild geese...

Byrne / Raftery (1924)

1. *Freshly caught Irish trout grilled over an open fire*

- **1 cleaned trout or other fish per serving**
- **1 sprig of fresh rosemary per fish**
- **14 g (1/2 oz) soft butter per fish**
- **a good pinch dried thyme and sage per fish**

Mix the dried herbs well into the butter. Coat the fish on each side with the herbed butter and set a sprig of rosemary on top. Grill over an open fire or barbecue for about 5 minutes on each side, basting once or twice more with the butter, until the skin is well browned and the fish is flaky.

2. An Irish Mixed Grill
Memories of my parents entertaining friends in the seventies, on late nights after I was long tucked up in bed, and the smells of an Irish Mixed Grill wafting up the stairs, still make my mouth water to this day.

Grill some **Irish bacon, Irish sausage, lamb chop cooked to a light brown (serve with chop bone decorated with paper frills), a choice piece of steak, thinly sliced lamb's liver, pork chop, vine tomatoes, fried potato bread or fried potatoes, sliced pineapple sautéed in brown sugar and butter, tinned or freshly cooked mushrooms sautéed gently in butter, baked beans, even add a fried hen or duck egg** if you like.

3. Pancakes Colleen

In the late 1970s Aer Lingus flights listed *Pancakes Colleen* on their first class menu as their special creation, and Irish cooks reproduced them according to taste in their own kitchens at home. They simply sautéed some **sliced mushrooms, shallots, prawns** and **shrimps in butter,** tossed them in **Lobster Sauce** (see Cú Chulainn Salmon recipe) to which was added a little **whiskey.** The original Aer Lingus menu described the sauce as *Sauce Americaine.* Lobster sauce was commonly used to recreate this at home in Ireland. The mixture was then served stuffed into **thinly made pancakes.**

4. Easy, Tasty Irish Stew

- 1 kg (2.2 lb) lamb chops, defrosted if frozen
- 1 kg (2.2 lb) diced casserole vegetables
- 4 large onions
- 2 sachets bouquet garni
- salt & pepper
- 1 kg (2.2 lb) peeled potatoes, cut in 2 if large

Put the lamb chops in a large saucepan and add enough water to cover the meat. Bring to the boil and peel and slice the onions. Add the bouquet garni, a layer of onions, then the vegetables, seasoning with salt and pepper as you go. Finally add the potatoes on top. Bring back to the boil and simmer for 1.5 to 2 hours.

5. Brown Stew

- 1350g (3 lb) potatoes (weight after peeling)
- 225g (1/2 lb) of steak pieces
- 225g (1/2 lb) minced steak
- 1 large carrot, sliced
- 1 large onion, chopped
- 2 of your favourite beef stock cubes
- salt & pepper
- about 1 litre boiling water

Brown the meat and onion. Cut any large potatoes in two, then combine all the ingredients in a large saucepan. Boil for 1.5 hours.

6. Irish Stout Stew

- **900g (2 lb) beef pieces**
- **1 sprig of fresh thyme or 1/2 teaspoon dried thyme**
- **4 medium sized onions, chopped**
- **2 cloves of garlic, finely chopped**
- **1 tablespoon sunflower oil**
- **500 ml Irish black stout**
- **1 tablespoon soft brown sugar**
- **1 bay leaf**
- **1 heaped tablespoon plain flour**
- **salt & pepper**

Heat the oil and fry the meat until brown. Set aside. Fry the onions and garlic until soft. Return the meat to the saucepan, stir in the flour, and gradually add the stout, stirring all the time until blended well. Add sugar and bring to simmering point. Add the thyme, bay leaf, salt and pepper. Put in a casserole dish and cook for about 2.5 hours at 150C / 300°F/ Gas Mark 2. Serve with Irish Colcannon.

7. Creamy Irish Colcannon Mash

Eliza Acton's Modern Cookery (1855) lists Colcannon as Kohl Cannon and Kale Cannon, and around 1774 the Irish comedian, Isaac Sparks, founded a Colcannon Club in Long Acre. (The Athenæum, January 20th, 1875). In Maria Edgeworth's Moral Tales Volume 1 (1816), Forester 'dined like a philosopher upon Colcannon'.

- **450 g (1 lb) cooked mashed potatoes, put through a potato ricer**
- **225 g (1/2 lb) finely chopped green cabbage and bacon, cooked**
- **1 teaspoon finely minced onion**
- **28 g (1 oz) country butter**
- **2 x 15 ml tablespoons fresh cream**
- **1/8 teaspoon pepper**
- **1/2 teaspoon salt**

Prepare the mashed potatoes. While still hot add the cooked chopped green cabbage and cooked chopped bacon. Melt the butter, add the onion, fresh cream, salt and pepper. Add the melted mixture to the potatoes, cabbage and bacon. Heat all well through together and serve very hot.

8. Salmon Frumenty

Poach **salmon** in **milk** with **a little onion, chopped parsley and a bayleaf.** Drain off milk and salmon juices and reserve. Melt **a little butter** in a saucepan, stir in **a tablespoon or two of cornflour / cornstarch** and mix well. Add reserved juices and milk and simmer to form a smooth sauce, whisking all the time. Add a little more milk if the sauce is too thick. Serve with the salmon on **a bed of creamy Irish Colcannon**. Season with **salt and pepper** and garnish with **chopped fresh parsley**.

9. Lamb Dinner by the Peat Turf Fire

- **lamb kidneys**
- **one large onion and one rasher of bacon for each lamb's kidney**
- **a little good quality stock**
- **salt & pepper**
- **creamy Colcannon to serve**

Season each lamb's kidney and roll in a rasher of bacon. Slice the top off each raw onion and make a cavity just big enough to hold the rolled kidneys. Set these into the cavities, drizzle with a little stock, and season well with salt and pepper. Replace the top of the stuffed onions, wrap in tinfoil and roast in the turf at the side of the fire or in a moderately hot oven 190C / 375F / Gas Mark 5. Serve with creamy Irish Colcannon and a thick rich dark gravy.

10. Fillet Steak in a Bramble Jus

A September recipe; the month of magical Irish morning mists, breathtaking western sunsets and hedgerows laden down with plump juicy blackberries.

serves two
- **4 small slices fillet steak**
- **a little sunflower oil**
- **150 ml beef stock**
- **2 tablespoons Cabernet Sauvignon red wine vinegar**
- **2 level teaspoons cornflour / cornstarch**
- **110 g (1/4 lb) fresh blackberries**
- **1 teaspoon honey**
- **ground black pepper**

Heat the sunflower oil in a frying pan and fry the fillet steak slices for several minutes on each side until cooked to your liking.

Remove steaks from the pan and set aside, leaving the sediment remaining in the frying pan.

Add the beef stock to the frying pan.

Blend the red wine vinegar with the cornflour and add to the beef stock.
Stir well and simmer until beginning to thicken.

Add the blackberries and simmer until most of the juice is released from the berries.

Put the mixture through a sieve and return to the pan. Add the honey and black pepper to taste.

Bring to a simmer again, warm the steak and serve with green vegetables and potatoes, and the sauce drizzled over the meat.

11. Scrambled Eggs with Irish Smoked Salmon

Use **2 large eggs** per person, whip up with **a little fresh milk**, season with **salt and pepper,** then scramble in a pan with **a little butter.** Serve with **sliced smoked Irish non-farmed salmon** and **fresh tossed salad leaves.**

12. Irish Salmon Fish Cakes

- **225 g (1/2 lb) fresh cooked Irish non-farmed salmon, flaked**
- **225 g (1/2 lb) boiled, mashed potatoes put through a potato ricer**
- **55 g (2 oz) butter**
- **2 eggs**
- **a small bowl of breadcrumbs**
- **salt and pepper**
- **oil for frying**
- **a little flour for rolling out**

Mix flaked salmon with the mashed potatoes and season to taste. Beat one of the eggs and add to the mixture along with the melted butter to bind. Roll out on a lightly floured worktop 4 cm / 1.5 inches thickness. Cut out into scone sized circles. Whip the second egg.
Dip the salmon cakes into the beaten egg, then the breadcrumbs. Fry until golden brown.

13. Vegetable Marrow Bake

- **1 kg (2.25 lb) grated vegetable marrow**
- **2 cloves garlic, finely chopped**
- **2 large eggs, at room temperature**
- **salt & pepper**
- **about a third of a nutmeg, freshly grated**
- **2 medium sized onions, finely chopped**
- **100 ml tomato juice**
- **55 g (2 oz) grated cheddar cheese**

Wash vegetable marrow and cut in half. Cut again in opposite direction, discarding middle pieces containing the seeds. Weigh out 1 kg (2.25lb) and grate. Put tomato juice, onions and garlic in a saucepan and cook until tender. Add grated marrow and cook for another 10 minutes. Add salt, pepper and grated nutmeg. Leave to cool down in a casserole dish. Whip eggs up until they froth. Pour over cooled vegetables. Sprinkle cheese over the top. Bake in a glass ovenproof dish at 170C / 325F / Gas Mark 3 for 20 minutes.

14. Wild Atlantic Seafood Crumble

- approximately 450g (1 lb) mixed Irish seafood, cubed
- 1 bay leaf
- 1 onion, chopped
- 280 ml (1/2 pint) milk
- 28g (1 oz) butter
- 28g (1 oz) plain flour
- freshly grated nutmeg to taste
- salt and pepper
- a small handful chopped fresh parsley
- 110g (4 oz) Irish cheddar cheese, grated
- 85g (3 oz) breadcrumbs

Preheat the oven to 350F / 180C / Gas Mark 4.

Poach the fish with the onion and the milk for about 5 minutes. Lift the fish and onion out with a strainer and set in a buttered ovenproof dish.

Using the milk that the fish has been poached in, make a roux sauce by melting the butter, beating in the flour and simmering with the leftover milk.

Add seasoning and parsley and stir in half of the cheese.

Mix the rest of the cheese with the breadcrumbs. Pour sauce over fish, sprinkle with the cheesy breadcrumbs and bake for half an hour.

15. Cú Chulainn Salmon

Named after one of Ireland's greatest mytholoical heroes, the legendary Cú Chulainn was famous for his salmon leaps.

- 2 x 170g (6 oz) non-farmed salmon steaks
- 1 egg
- breadcrumbs
- a little butter
- the juice of half a lemon
- 55g (2oz) sliced mushrooms, sautéed in a little butter
- 6 king prawns, sautéed in butter
- Emer's sauce
- Lobster sauce

(15b) Emer's Sauce

- **3 tablespoons water**
- **3 tablespoons tarragon vinegar**
- **1/2 medium onion**
- **4 egg yolks, lightly beaten**
- **1/2 teaspoon salt**
- **1/8 teaspoon paprika**
- **4 tablespoons butter, creamed**

Put water, vinegar and onion in a small saucepan and bring to boiling point. Remove onion. Gradually add egg yolks and mix in seasonings. Strain through a sieve. Cook in a double saucepan over hot water until beginning to thicken. Add butter, 1 tablespoon at a time, stirring continuously.

(15c) Lobster Sauce

- **2 tablespoons butter**
- **3 tablespoons plain flour**
- **235 ml lobster stock**
- **1/4 teaspoon salt**
- **80 ml cup cream**
- **a good handful diced cooked lobster**
- **2 eggs yolks, lightly beaten**

Make lobster stock by boiling the body, bones and claws of a lobster and seasoning it with salt, paprika and lemon juice. Melt the butter, add flour and seasonings, stir until well blended. Add lobster stock slowly, stirring constantly. Bring to boiling point. Boil for two minutes. Add cream and egg yolks. Simmer out for a minute or so, then add the diced cooked lobster.

To cook the Cú Chulainn Salmon

Dip the salmon steaks in whisked egg and breadcrumbs. Cook in the butter and lemon juice. Set on serving dish topped with the sautéed mushroom and prawns. Mix the Lobster sauce and Emer's sauce well together well and serve in a sauce boat, or pour over the dressed salmon steaks to glaze.

16. Skellig Islands Trout

- **6 medium trout**
- **1 litre Irish ale**
- **225 g (8 oz) small shallots**
- **335 g (12 oz) button mushrooms**
- **225 g (8 oz) baby carrots**
- **225g (8 oz) cooked garden peas**
- **about 110g (4 oz) butter**
- **2 tablespoons cornflour / corn starch**
- **2 bay leaves**
- **small bunch of thyme**
- **salt & pepper**
- **caramel browning**
- **chopped parsley**

Put the prepared trout in a large pan with a few knobs of butter, the bay leaves and thyme. Cover with the ale and poach gently.

Meanwhile sauté the shallots, mushrooms and baby carrots separately in a little butter. Add a few tablespoons of the fish cooking liquid to each vegetable to cook out. When the trout is nicely cooked, drain off the cooking liquid into a separate saucepan, removing the herbs. Add any liquid that is left from the cooked vegetables. Simmer gently to reduce the liquid down a little. In a separate pan melt the remainder of the butter (about 55g /2 oz), add the cornflour and whisk in the slightly reduced cooking liquid. Season well and colour with a little caramel browning if liked.

Reheat the fish and vegetables and serve with the sauce and some creamy Colcannon or fresh crusty bread.

17. Fillet of Sole with Irish Dulse Seaweed

- **4 small handfuls of dulse Irish seaweed**
- **4 fillets of sole**
- **55g (2 oz) butter + a little extra for the dulse and to glaze the sole**
- **4 potatoes**
- **a little plain flour**
- **sunflower oil for deep frying**
- **a few sprigs of parsley**

Wash the dulse well in cold water. Simmer gently for an hour in water, stock or milk. Drain well, mix a good knob of country butter through the dulse and set aside.

Peel and slice the potatoes thickly and deep fry.

Meanwhile dip the sole fillets in flour and shallow fry gently in the butter.

To serve, warm the dulse and arrange on a large serving dish. Lay the fried potato slices around the sides of the dish and lay the fillets of sole on top of the bed of dulse.

Pour a little sizzled golden butter over fish and decorate with sprigs of parsley.

18. Atlantic Coast Seafood Tian
Serves 4

- **4 heaped tablespoons homemade fairly stiff potato salad**
- **small bunch chives – finely chopped (keep a few aside for decoration)**
- **225g (1/2 lb) cooked Irish crab meat**
- **225g (1/2 lb) Irish smoked salmon, chopped (reserve a little to decorate)**
- **125 ml (about 8 tablespoons) crème fraiche**
- **1 or 2 teaspoons brandy**

Place ring moulds onto individual serving plates. Place a tablespoon of the potato salad into each mould and smooth until level.

Sprinkle an even layer of chopped chives all over the top of the potato.

Mix the crab meat with a little brandy and enough crème fraiche to bind together. Spoon one quarter of this mixture into each of the moulds, and press down until level. Next divide the chopped smoked salmon in 4 and place a layer on top of the dressed crab meat.

Leave to set in the fridge. Gently remove from the mould and top carefully with a little crème fraiche, small ribbons of smoked salmon and chopped chives. Serve with tossed salad leaves.

19. Dublin Bay Prawn Cocktail

Ingredients for one serving
- **6 cooked and shelled King prawns**
- **small handful of shredded iceberg lettuce**
- **1 tablespoon finely chopped celery**
- **salt & ground white pepper**

Sauce:
- **2 tablespoons whipped double cream**
- **1/2 teaspoon white malt vinegar**
- **1/3 teaspoon Worcestershire sauce**
- **a little freshly squeezed lemon juice, sieved**
- **2 teaspoons tomato ketchup**
- **½ teaspoon horseradish sauce**
- **salt and pepper**

Mix all the sauce ingredients together, then mix in the prawns, reserving one or two to decorate glass if wished. Leave to chill in the fridge. Mix the lettuce with the chopped celery and season well. Put into a cocktail glass. Arrange the prawn cocktail on top. Serve sprinkled with finely chopped parsley.

20. Dublin Rarebit

- **110g (4 oz) Irish cheddar cheese, grated**
- **1 egg yolk**
- **1 teaspoon Worcestershire sauce**
- **1 level teaspoon mustard**
- **1 tablespoon Irish stout**
- **butter, at room temperature**
- **2 or 3 slices bread**

Mix cheese, egg yolk, mustard and stout well together. Butter bread on both sides. Divide mixture evenly over each slice of bread. Bake, grill or cook over an open fire until bubbling hot and browned. Season to taste.

21. Traditional Dublin Bacon Coddle

- **500 g (1.2 lb) thick bacon misshapes / cooking bacon**
- **340 g (3/4 lb) best quality Irish pork sausages**
- **2 large onions, sliced**
- **4 large potatoes, peeled and sliced**
- **1 chicken stock cube**
- **2 bay leaves**
- **950 ml boiling water**
- **a little vegetable oil**
- **a little finely chopped parsley to garnish**

Cut the bacon into cubes, cover with the water, chicken stock cube and bay leaves and simmer for 45 minutes.
Skim off any scum and lift out bacon pieces, still reserving the water.
Cut the sausages into chunks and flash fry for 3-5 minutes in a little vegetable oil.
Put the sliced potatoes and sliced onions into the bacon water. Add the sausage chunks and bacon and simmer for about half an hour, until cooked. Remove the bay leaves.
Serve out and sprinkle each serving with a little finely chopped parsley. This adds flavour and colour, don't omit it if at all possible.

22. Stuffed Sausages

- **6 Irish pork sausages**
- **6 slices of bacon**
- **6 heaped tablespoons breadcrumbs**
- **1 onion, chopped finely and sautéed in a little butter**
- **1 dessertspoon finely chopped parsley**

Preheat oven to 190C / 375F / Gas Mark 5.
Mix sautéed onion with parsley and breadcrumbs. Make a cut nearly the length of each sausage, leaving a little bit uncut at each end. Open them out a little and fill the cavity with stuffing. Stretch the bacon and wrap a slice round each stuffed sausage. Bake for 25 – 35 minutes until cooked through.

A writer in 'The Irish Society Review' September 24, 1904 reminisced about Belleek in County Fermanagh, where a little hotel on the banks of the River Erne kept fresh live eels in a tank outside, ready for the chef to cook up for the evening menu. 'I well remember once staying at the hotel at Belleek and asking the proprietor if he had any eels left in his tank, and whether he would let us have some for dinner. He at once went with me to catch the fish and it was cooked for the "table d'hote" dinner. When handed round the eels looked like filleted soles. Everybody partook of the dish and then looked up with curiosity to learn what it really was. Greatly amused, I said, "The fact is I asked for some Ballyshannon eels and here they are!" One of the gentlemen present, an angler from London, who evidently felt himself an authority, observed: "They are very good, but not as good as London eels." I ventured to suggest that the London eel was only an Irish silver eel, three days old, instead of quite fresh, which was the fact.'

23. Lough Erne Eel Pie

from 'Dreams & Recipes 1904 - 1914'

- **2 eels**
- **55g (2 oz) butter**
- **240ml sherry**
- **120ml Harvey's sauce (next recipe)**
- **6 mushrooms, chopped**
- **1 shallot, chopped**
- **bunch of parsley**
- **28g (1 oz) plain flour**
- **½ a lemon**
- **3 eggs, hard boiled and cut into quarters**
- **seasonings – nutmeg & cayenne pepper**
- **rich pastry for the pie crust**

Cleanse and prepare 2 good-sized eels in the normal manner. Cut them in 7.5 cm / 3 inch lengths and put them in a stew pan with the fresh butter, sherry and Harvey's sauce. Add barely enough water to cover. Next add the chopped mushrooms, parsley, pepper, salt, nutmeg, and the chopped shallot. Bring to the boil, then take out the pieces of eel and put them in a pie dish. Thicken the sauce with flour and stir till it boils. Add lemon juice and cayenne, then pour the sauce over the eels in the pie dish.
Cover this with the quartered hard boiled eggs.
Roll out the pastry to form a pie crust.
Bake for about 1 hour at 190C / 375F / Gas Mark 5 and serve hot or cold.

24. Harvey's Sauce

- **475 ml strong vinegar**
- **6 anchovies**
- **2 heads garlic (all the cloves in a garlic bulb)**
- **90 ml soy sauce**
- **90 ml mushroom ketchup**
- **1.5 teaspoons cayenne pepper**
- **red food colouring**

Mash and dissolve the anchovies in the vinegar then stir in the soy sauce, mushroom ketchup and cayenne pepper.

Divide the garlic cloves, peel and then chop them finely before adding to the vinegar mix.

Add a few drops of red colouring then put into a large, sterilized jar.

Leave to infuse in the vinegar for 2 weeks, shaking each day.

At the end of this time strain the liquid and pour into sterilized bottles with air-tight corks.

25. Donegal Pie Recipe

- **2 hard-boiled eggs**
- **6 potatoes, boiled**
- **1 tablespoon minced fresh parsley**
- **1 tablespoon finely chopped fresh chives**
- **4 rashers of bacon**
- **170 g (6 oz) ready-made shortcrust pastry**

Fry the bacon and chop it into small pieces, reserving the bacon fat. Mash the potatoes, put through a potato ricer to make smooth, then mix in the parsley and chives. Butter a deep ovenproof pie dish and lay just over half of the hot freshly mashed potatoes along the base, pressing down evenly with a fork. Cover with a layer of sliced hard-boiled eggs, then cover with a layer of the crisp bacon, sprinkling the reserved bacon fat across top of pie. Then fill up with the rest of the mashed potatoes and cover with a lid of shortcrust pastry. Cook at 350°F/ 180°C / Gas Mark 4 until golden.

26. Donegal Crab Quiche

- **225g (1/2 lb) cooked crabmeat**
- **ready-made rough puff pastry, at room temperature**
- **1 egg white**
- **1 tablespoon finely chopped celery**
- **2 tablespoons finely chopped parsley or dill**
- **140ml (1/4 pint) cider**
- **salt and pepper**
- **5 large eggs**
- **284 ml single cream**
- **150 ml milk**
- **135 g finely grated Gruyère cheese**
- **a grating of nutmeg**

Line a quiche dish with the pastry and chill in the fridge for 1 hour. When chilled, lightly brush pastry with egg white. Flake the crab meat and lay across the pastry base followed by celery, parsley, cider and seasoning. Beat eggs, cream and milk together add a grating of nutmeg and the grated cheese, then carefully pour over the quiche. Bake at 200C / 400F /Gas Mark 6 for the first 10 minutes, then reduce heat a little and bake for another 20 minutes or so until cooked through.

27. Lobster Cream

- **1 cooked lobster**
- **450g (1 lb) whiting, cooked**
- **285 ml (1/2 pint) cream, whipped**
- **140 ml fish stock**
- **1 egg**
- **40g (1.5 oz) butter**
- **55g (2 oz) plain flour**
- **salt, pepper, lemon juice and fish sauce**
- **a drop or two of natural red colouring (if desired)**

Rub the whiting through a sieve.
Make a roux sauce with the butter, flour and fish stock, season to taste.
Blend in a mortar, (or whizz in a food processor for a few seconds), whiting, lemon juice, fish sauce, some of the lobster, shredded, and the egg.

Fold in the whipped cream. Add a drop or two of natural red colouring at this point, if desired.

Butter some dariole moulds, or a soufflé mould, put a little greaseproof paper in the bottom, put in the claws and the nicest parts of the lobster, and then add the soufflé mixture.

Cover with greaseproof paper, and steam gently for one hour (1/2 hour for dariole moulds).

Sauce

- **28g (1 oz) plain flour**
- **28g (1 oz) butter**
- **284 ml (1/2 pint) fish stock**
- **4 x 15 ml tablespoons cream**
- **salt & pepper**
- **lemon juice to taste**

Blend together flour and butter, add stock, and stir till it boils.
Then add cream, salt, pepper and lemon juice.

28. Fish Mould

- **450g (1 lb) cooked mixed fish, flaked (smoked cod, haddock, salmon)**
- **110g (4 oz) long grain rice, cooked**
- **1 dessertspoon chopped parsley (or 1 teaspoon vegetable Bouillon powder)**
- **1/2 teaspoon salt**
- **1/4 teaspoon pepper**
- **2 eggs**
- **28g (1oz) butter**
- **120 ml milk**

Mix all the dry ingredients together.

Beat eggs well, add milk and then the butter, melted.

Steam in a buttered mould (or in a 2.5 pint/ 1.4 litre ovenproof glass pudding bowl) covered with tinfoil for 45 minutes in the oven at approximately 200C / 400F / Gas Mark 6.

Turn out and serve with the following sauce poured around :-

28b. Boiled Mayonnaise Sauce

- **2 yolks of eggs, raw**
- **1 teaspoon mustard**
- **1 dessertspoon tarragon vinegar**
- **1 dessertspoon common vinegar**
- **1 dessertspoon salad oil**
- **235 ml cream**
- **salt & pepper**

Beat yolks slightly; add all the ingredients except for the cream; beat again, add cream, and boil in a double saucepan, stirring constantly till it thickens.

29. Leitrim Brawn Recipe

- **1 pig's head**
- **2 pig's tongues**
- **2 pig's feet**
- **2 extra pig's ears**
- **4 dry-cured sausages**
- **some slices of boiled ox tongue**
- **1 teaspoon sage**
- **1 teaspoon salt**
- **1 teaspoon pepper**
- **a few tablespoons of salt to cover the pig's head**

Wash the pig's head well in warm water. Rub the head all over with salt and leave to lie for three days. Then put it in a large saucepan with cold water. Bring to the boil and let it cook away gently, or until is soft, and the bones come away easily. This may take about six hours. Meanwhile boil the 2 tongues, feet and ears for 1.5 hours. Strain the stock from both saucepans and reserve. Leave pig's head to get cold then take out the bones. Cut all the meat into small pieces. Season with sage, salt and pepper. Cut the sausages into slices. Take a mould or tin and place slices of ox tongue in a pattern round it, fill up with the meat, add a small amount of stock to moisten but do not make it too damp. Press down firmly with a weight and leave to stand overnight in a cold place.

30. Craiceann

Pronounced as "crac-enn" with the "r" rolled slightly in Ulster, "crac-in" in Connacht, and "cric-en" in Munster, Craiceann is the Irish word for peel, rind, skin or husks and really a little bit of everything good that was to hand went into this dish.

- approximately 4 litres water
- bone and shin of beef
- 3 large onions
- 5 shallots
- a few cloves of garlic
- 3 whole leeks
- 5 carrots
- 3 parsnips
- 1 turnip
- 1 curly cabbage
- 170 g (6 oz) barley meal
- 110 g (4 oz) fine oatmeal
- a good handful of elderberries
- 2 mugs filled with young nettle tops
- a good handful of sorrel
- a good handful watercress
- 3 bay leaves
- salt & pepper to taste

Cut all vegetables up into small pieces. Put into a large pot with bone and shin of beef and simmer slowly for 3 to 4 hours.

Serve with thick slices of wheaten bread generously spread with **butter.**

31. Old Dublin Seafood Salad

Take some cooked cockles and mussels, sliced tomatoes, hard-boiled eggs, cucumber and **chopped beetroot** and arrange on a bed of **crisp lettuce.**
Sprinkle over with your favourite **French dressing** and **finely chopped onion.**

32. Anraith an Lae - Soup of the Day

- **1.4 kg (3 lb) shin of beef, on the bone OR 1 kg (2.2 lb) of steak pieces**
- **2 litres water**
- **4 carrots**
- **1 large leek**
- **1 large onion**
- **small bunch of curly parsley**
- **small bunch of leaf celery**
- **a little handful of dried soup mix**
- **a few potatoes to add in the last hour of cooking**
- **salt & pepper**
- **a few drops of Yorkshire Relish or Worcestershire sauce to taste**
- **1 tablespoon brown sugar**

Fry the beef for a few minutes in a frying pan to brown the outside. Put beef in a large saucepan with the water and simmer for about half an hour. Add rest of ingredients apart from the potatoes, seasoning and sugar. Simmer for around 2 hours, add potatoes and simmer for 1 more hour until all is cooked nicely. Some Irish cooks leave the beef on the bone, others remove the beef shin, take the meat from the bones and return meat to the saucepan. Add seasoning to taste. Brown a tablespoon of brown sugar gently in a pan and add this to the soup just before serving. Stir well to give the soup a nice colour.

33. Irish Nettle & Oatmeal Broth

- **2 onions, finely chopped**
- **55g (2 oz) butter**
- **1700 ml good quality stock**
- **1700 ml container full of young nettle-tops, finely chopped**
- **85g (3 oz) pinhead oatmeal OR 85g (3 oz) flaked oats**
- **1 finely chopped leek**
- **salt, pepper and grated nutmeg to season**
- **120 ml cream**
- **1 egg yolk**

Sweat chopped onion, nettle leaves and leek in the butter. Add oatmeal and stock and simmer for about 45 minutes. Just before serving, adjust the seasoning, very lightly whip the cream with the egg yolk and swirl this through the soup.

34. Vine Tomatoes stuffed with Irish Smoked Salmon

- **6 Irish home-grown vine tomatoes**
- **55g (2 oz) smoked Irish salmon, chopped**
- **28g (1 oz) butter**
- **1/2 medium onion, finely chopped**
- **fresh parsley, chopped finely**
- **salt and pepper**
- **freshly squeezed lemon juice**
- **sunflower oil cooking spray**

Mix the salmon with the butter, onion and a little chopped parsley. Cut a slice from the top of each tomato and reserve. Remove pulp and seeds. Season the tomato cases with salt, pepper and a little freshly squeezed lemon juice. Fill them with the smoked salmon mixture. Grill, oven bake or cook in an Airfryer until heated well through.

35. Belfast Chip Shop Pastie Recipe

Belfast's Van Morrison sings of Belfast chip shop pasties in 'A Sense of Wonder'. You can still order a Pastie Supper in most traditional Belfast chip shops. Different from a Cornish pasty, Belfast Pasties look just like a battered sausage, only in the shape of a burger.

- **450g (1 lb) Irish pork sausagemeat**
- **85g (3 oz) fresh white breadcrumbs**
- **225g (8 oz) cooked, mashed potato**
- **1/2 teaspoon salt**
- **1/2 teaspoon ground white pepper**
- **1/2 teaspoon monosodium glutamate**
- **2 teaspoons Worcester sauce**
- **1 teaspoon ground coriander**
- **1/2 teaspoon freshly grated nutmeg**
- **60 ml water**
- **1 medium onion, finely chopped**

Batter

- **55g (2 oz) self raising flour**
- **½ teaspoon salt**
- **120 ml milk**
- **1 egg, lightly beaten**

Combine all pastie ingredients together.

Form into plump burger shapes about 8.5cm / 3.5 inches in diameter.

Combine batter ingredients together. Dip pasties in batter, and deep fry at 190C until cooked through.

Sprinkle with salt and vinegar and serve with chips or mashed potatoes and vegetables.

36. Homemade Sausage Rolls

- **110g (1/4 lb) ready-made puff pastry**
- **140g (5 oz) Irish sausage meat**
- **a little chicken or vegetable stock**
- **1 egg, whipped**

Roll the pastry out thinly into 7.5 cm / 3 inch wide strips. Mix just enough stock through sausage meat to give a pipeable consistency.

Using a round plain piping nozzle pipe a thin rope of sausagemeat down the centre of the pastry strips. Moisten the edges of the pastry with a little water, then fold over the filling mixture and seal the edges. Cut into individual portions, brush tops of pastry with a little whipped egg, and put on a baking tray lined with baking paper.

Leave to rest for 15 minutes, then bake at 400F /200C / gas Mark 6 for 20 minutes until well cooked.

37. Belfast Batch Bread Snacks

A vintage supper snack recipe made using the big square unsliced white batch bread that's still produced in Irish bakeries today.

- 225g (8 oz) cold, cooked fish, bones removed
- 28g (1 oz) butter
- 28g (1 oz) plain flour
- 140 ml (1/4 pint) milk
- 3 slices cut from unsliced batch loaf bread, about 4 cm / 1.5 inches thick
- 1/2 teaspoon salt
- 1/4 teaspoon pepper
- beaten egg to coat bread
- lard for frying

Cut rounds from each slice of bread. Scoop out a little in the centre of each. Brush each with beaten egg, fry in hot lard, drain.

Season the flour with the salt and pepper. Melt butter, add flour and combine. Whisk in the milk and heat to make a thick sauce, whisking all the time. Add flaked fish, beat thoroughly, and pile mixture up in the centre of each round.

38. Prátaí Inis Ceithleann

Irish potatoes sliced and slowly baked in milk, cream, garlic and cheese, a favourite restaurant side dish in my hometown of Enniskillen.

- **1.5 kg (3.4 lb) peeled potatoes**
- **560 ml (1 pint) milk**
- **280 ml (1/2 pint) double cream**
- **55g (2 oz) butter, melted (+ extra to grease dishes)**
- **1/2 teaspoon ground nutmeg**
- **4 cloves garlic**
- **grated cheddar cheese to sprinkle on top**

In a bowl combine milk, cream, melted butter and finely chopped garlic. Slice peeled potatoes very thinly. Arrange potato slices in individual ovenproof dishes (buttered well first) or one large oven proof dish. Pour milk and cream mixture over to cover . Cover with lid or tin foil and bake at 300F/150C/Gas Mark 2 for 45 minutes. Remove from oven and sprinkle with cheese. Do not cover. Return to oven for a further 45 minutes or until potatoes are tender and cheese is golden. Serve bubbling hot .

39. Atlantic Herring Log

- **450g (1 lb) Irish sea herrings, cooked and bones removed**
- **70g (2.5 oz) white breadcrumbs**
- **2 eggs**
- **140 ml (1/4 pint) milk**
- **1 teaspoon fresh lemon juice**
- **1/2 teaspoon salt**
- **1/4 teaspoon ground white pepper**
- **1/2 teaspoon dried sage**
- **small onion finely chopped**
- **1 tablespoon chopped fresh parsley**

Put the breadcrumbs in a bowl and add eggs and milk. Mix in fish, lemon juice, seasonings, sage, chopped onion and parsley. Pack into a well-greased deep loaf tin. Bake at 325° F / 170°C, Gas Mark 3 for about three quarters of an hour until the log is firm and golden. Serve with buttered carrots and brown bread.

40. Meatloaf

- **670g (1.5 lb) minced beef**
- **2 tablespoons tomato ketchup**
- **110g (4 oz) brown breadcrumbs**
- **1 medium onion, chopped and fried**
- **1 rounded teaspoon herbs de Provence**
- **55g (2 oz) crème fraiche**
- **salt and pepper**
- **225g (8 oz) sausagemeat or skinned sausages**
- **2 beaten eggs**
- **1 large Bramley cooking apple, grated**
- **1 tablespoon chopped fresh parsley**
- **¼ teaspoon nutmeg**
- **2 cloves garlic, finely chopped (optional)**
- **a good shake of all purpose savoury seasoning**

Mix all the ingredients together in a large bowl. Form into the shape of a loaf and place on an open non-stick baking tray.
Cover with grease-proof paper. Bake for 1.5 hours at 375 F / 190 C / Gas Mark 4 -5. Serve with side salad and baked potatoes.

41. Old-fashioned Stuffing Recipe

Take 110g (1/4 lb) **bread crumbs**, 110g (1/4 lb) **chopped suet**, as much **chopped parsley** as will lie on a tablespoon, about a spoonful chopped **sweet marjoram**, and **a little grated lemon peel, pepper, and salt.** Mix all these thoroughly together with **one beaten egg and a little sweet milk.** This forms a dough sufficient for a small turkey or large fowl.

42. Irish Hotch Potch

- **670g (1.5 lb) lean neck of mutton or lamb**
- **3 small turnips**
- **3 carrots**
- **3 onions**
- **1400 ml water**
- **1/2 a lettuce**
- **1/2 a cauliflower**
- **280g (10 oz) green peas**
- **a small handful of chopped parsley**
- **salt to taste**

Put half the meat in a large saucepan, bring to the boil , add salt and skim carefully as it boils. Boil for one hour; meanwhile cut remainder of meat into small chops; dice the turnips, carrots, and onions, and add meat and diced vegetables along with half the peas when the one hour is up. Boil for a further half an hour. Chop up the lettuce, divide cauliflower in sprigs, chop parsley, and add to the soup with the rest of the peas; boil for a further half hour; season and serve.

43. Poached Cod Roes (an old Bangor recipe)
Cod roes are delicious poached or fried, but are a lot more expensive to buy than they used to be.

Drop some **cod roes** into boiling water, to which has been added one table-spoonful of **vinegar,** and one of **salt**. Boil till quite firm, drain, and set aside to cool. When cold, cut into 1.25 cm / 1/2 inch slices. In a saucepan put 28g (1 oz) **butter**, and, when melted, stir in two beaten **eggs**, a little **salt, pepper, cayenne, grate of nutmeg,** and 1 dessertspoonful of **tomato sauce**. Mix all together, and stir over the heat till it thickens - dip in, one at a time, the slices of roe. Arrange on a dish, pour over remainder of sauce, and place in oven for a few minutes; serve very hot.

44. Old Belfast recipe for Chicken Omelette

- **21g (3/4 oz) butter**
- **3 eggs whisked with 1 tablespoon milk**
- **salt and pepper**
- **about 55g (2 ozs) leftover cold cooked chicken**
- **a little white sauce**

Remove all skin from the remains of chicken, and cut into small pieces. Put into small saucepan, with sauce; heat through thoroughly; season carefully. Whisk the eggs well with the milk and a little salt; melt the butter in an omelette pan; when the butter is hot, pour in egg and cook gently till the eggs begin to set. Then pour hot chicken and sauce inside the centre; fold the omelette over into a neat oval shape, let brown slightly. Serve at once.

45. Smoked Haddock & Cheese Savoury
Crab or kippers may also be cooked in this way.

- **1 smoked haddock (raw)**
- **55g (2 oz) grated cheese**
- **30 ml cream**
- **a little mustard**
- **pinch of cayenne**
- **1 egg**
- **hot buttered toast to serve**

Scrape the fish from the bone, and mix it with the other ingredients. Cook this for a few minutes, then add a beaten up egg, and boil the mixture for another few minutes until cooked through. Serve on hot buttered toast.

46. Promisques (an old breakfast dish)

Peel some **hard boiled eggs** (as many as required - one egg makes two promisques), cut each egg in half long ways ; roll round each half egg a piece of **bacon**; dip each one in an ordinary **fritter batter**, and fry in **deep fat** till a nice golden brown colour.

47. Eggs Prince Congal

From the old Irish tale of Prince Congal, who on sitting down to a feast, was enraged to find his egg had taken the form of a hen egg, whilst the Princes around him were enjoying goose eggs. This recipe is traditionally made in Ireland with either blue duck eggs or newly laid goose eggs.

- **12 ready-made baked puff pastry boats**
- **6 goose or duck eggs, hard-boiled**
- **140 ml cream**
- **1 finely minced shallot**
- **fresh parsley, chervil, tarragon and celery leaf, finely chopped**
- **juice of half a lemon**
- **salt**
- **watercress salad to serve**

Cut hard-boiled eggs lengthways and remove yolks. Set egg white bases aside on a plate. Sieve the yolks and add the rest of the ingredients, mixing well. Transfer mixture to a piping bag fitted with a rosette nozzle. Pipe a little of mixture into each pastry boat and lay an egg white base on top of each one. Pipe a rosette of mixture into each yolk cavity and sprinkle with a little finely chopped parsley to garnish. Serve on a bed of watercress salad.

48. Gaelic Steak

per portion-
- **1 fillet steak**
- **28g (1 oz) butter**
- **2 tablespoons cream**
- **2 tablespoons Irish whiskey**

Fry steak in melted butter. Remove from pan and drain. Pour cream and whiskey into pan, stir and heat, then pour over steak and serve immediately with market vegetables and baby potatoes.

49. *Fillet of Beef*

- **450g (1 lb) beef fillet**
- **1 large onion**
- **a little butter**
- **1 tablespoon mustard**
- **30 ml brown vinegar**
- **60 ml tomato ketchup**
- **90 ml claret**
- **salt & pepper**
- **280 ml (1/2 pint) brown stock**
- **a little cornflour to thicken**

Butter an ovenproof dish. Thinly slice onion into it; lay the fillet on this, with a nice bit of butter over it, mustard, brown vinegar, ketchup, claret; salt and pepper. Cook for 45 minutes; baste it well. Strain the gravy into 280 ml (half pint) of good brown stock; season to taste (if necessary thicken with a little cornflour dissolved in a little cold water), and serve round the fillet.

50. *Galantine of Rabbit*

- **1 rabbit**
- **2 hard-boiled eggs**
- **110g (1/4 lb) cooked bam**
- **14g (1/2 oz) leaf gelatine**
- **salt & pepper**
- **30 ml vinegar**

Put the rabbit in water for two hours, cut up in joints, put into saucepan, cover with water, and vinegar, season well with salt and pepper. Let it stew until it frees the bones. Cut meat into pieces, put bones back into saucepan with the gelatine, and simmer half an hour. Cut the eggs into slices, and the ham into small pieces. Put rabbit, bam, and eggs into a pie-dish in layers, strain sauce on to top, keeping back one teacupful. Turn out next day, and garnish with parsley and the teacupful of sauce, which has now formed a jelly, chopped up.

51. Little Pheasant Creams

Take the meat off a **lightly roasted plump pheasant**, free from skin and bone (leave the legs, which will do for a grill). Put meat four times through a mining machine; flavour well with **salt and white pepper**. Mix all with about an equal quantity of **stiffly whipped cream**. Have ready 18 **paper ramekin cases**, place a slice of **tomato and cucumber** in each, then fill with pheasant cream; garnish with edging of squares of **tomato,** and on top of each cream place a small star cut from green peel of the cucumber. Arrange on a serving dish on lace paper.

52. Creamy Cider Trout

- **4 fillets of Irish rainbow trout**
- **finely shredded leeks**
- **diced carrots**
- **500 ml fish stock with enough cider added to flavour stock nicely**
- **a little cornflour dissolved in water to thicken**
- **a good dash of cream**
- **the yolk of an egg**
- **watercress to decorate**

Poach the trout, leeks and carrots in the cider and fish stock. When cooked drain the stock and reserve it. Arrange the trout on a bed of the carrots and leeks. Slightly thicken the stock with a little cornflour, mix in the egg yolk, cook for another minute, add cream, then glaze the trout with the sauce. Garnish with a little watercress.

53. Fish Steamed Between Two Plates

Take **a fillet of lemon sole or plaice** and remove the black skin. Wash and dry the fish. **Butter** a plate well and set the fish on it. Season with **salt & pepper and a little lemon juice**. Add a dab or two of butter, and a tablespoon of **milk**. Put another plate over the top and cook over a saucepan (of a size to fit the plates) of boiling water. Cook for 20 minutes, turning the fish once.

54. Tomato Sauce

- 28g (1 oz) butter
- 28g (1 oz) rice flour
- 28g (1 oz) lean ham
- piece of carrot, turnip, onion, celery, all cut very small
- bunch of herbs
- 5 tomatoes
- 280 ml (1/2 pint) stock
- 140 ml (1/4 pint) tomato juice
- salt & pepper
- lemon juice
- 1 teaspoonful of sugar

Melt butter and fry the vegetables cut small, bunch of herbs, tomatoes well broken up; sprinkle in rice flour, then stock and liquor; simmer for thirty minutes, then pass through a sieve, and stir in pepper, salt, lemon juice, and sugar.

55. Marrow Dumplings for Soups & Broths

- 110g (4 oz) beef marrow, minced
- 110g (4 oz) fine breadcrumbs
- 2 eggs, whisked
- salt & pepper
- finely chopped parsley

Mix beef marrow with the breadcrumbs, salt and pepper and chopped parsley. Bind together with whisked eggs. Chill in the fridge for about an hour. Form into dumpling balls and add to simmering broth 12 minutes before serving.

56. Nettle Stuffing

- 110g (4 oz) white breadcrumbs
- 55g (2 oz) young nettle-tops, chopped
- 1 heaped tablespoon chopped onion
- 28g (1 oz) lard
- 1 egg

Cook the chopped onion in the lard until tender, but do not brown. Remove

61. Pan Seared Breast of Pheasant

- pheasant breast from wild pheasant that has been well hung
- butter
- a small bouquet of herbs
- 1 beaten egg
- well seasoned breadcrumbs

Preheat oven to 200C / 400F / Gas Mark 6. Cut pheasant breast in 2 and brown off nicely in pan with butter and herbs. Remove pheasant from pan, brush with beaten egg and dip in seasoned breadcrumbs. Place on a lightly greased ovenproof dish and bake for about 15 minutes until cooked through. Serve with seasonal vegetables and Scallion Champ.

62. Scallion Champ

- 670g (1.5 lb) freshly cooked potatoes, mashed and put through a ricer
- 28g (1oz) scallions (spring onions), finely chopped
- 40g (1.5 oz) butter
- 140 ml boiling milk
- salt & pepper
- a little more butter
- a little more milk

Preheat oven to 200C / 400F /Gas Mark 6. Fry the scallions gently in the butter. Add boiling milk and cook for 5 minutes. Add warm mashed potato, season with salt and pepper and combine all well together. Transfer to a buttered casserole dish, smooth out and dot over with a little butter on top. Sprinkle a little fresh milk over top and bake in oven until slightly brown.

63. Lentil Irish Stew

- 55g (2oz) butter
- small grated onion
- 225g (8 oz) lentils
- 850 ml (1.5 Imperial pints) hot water
- 1 grated carrot
- 450g (1 lb) peeled, sliced potatoes
- seasoning

49

Melt butter, add grated onion and lentils. Add hot water, grated carrot and sliced potatoes. Cook over a low heat for 1 hour. Season to taste before serving.

64. Ragout of Mutton
This dish also works well with stewing beef

225g (8 oz) mutton, cut into small cubes
2 tablespoons mushroom soup powder mix
2 tablespoons flour
28g (1 oz) dripping
3 carrots, peeled and sliced
1 onion, sliced
280 ml (1/2 pint) good stock

Roll the cubed mutton in the soup powder and flour.
Fry the sliced onion in the dripping, remove and fry the mutton until brown. Add onions, carrots and stock. Simmer for 2.5 hours. Serve with creamed potatoes.

65. Dun Laoghaire Fried Plaice
serves 2

1 whole plaice, skinned and filleted into 2 halves
salt & freshly ground black pepper
1 tablespoon plain flour
40g (1.5 oz) breadcrumbs
1 small egg
oil for frying
lemon slices
2 small sprigs parsley
2 knobs of parsley butter to serve

Wipe the plaice. Season the flour with salt and pepper. Beat the egg and coat the fish in it. Lightly coat the fillets in the seasoned flour, then fry gently for about 5 minutes on each side until the fish is cooked through and the coating is crisp. Garnish with parsley butter, lemon slice and sprig of parsley and serve with chips or creamed potatoes and Minted Peas.

66. Minted Peas

My Great-Aunt Ethel lived in Malahide, Co. Dublin. Her suburban townhouse had a long narrow back garden, filled with every fresh herb imaginable.

- **450g (1 lb) fresh home-grown peas**
- **1 sprig of fresh mint**
- **1/2 teaspoon caster sugar**
- **28g (1 oz) home-churned butter**

Shell the peas and wash the mint. Bring a saucepan of lightly salted water to the boil. Add the peas, sugar and half of the sprig of mint. Simmer until the peas are tender. Chop the rest of the mint, drain the peas, and sauté in butter with the chopped mint for a few minutes. Bring to table in a warmed serving dish.

67. Parsley Butter

- **55g (2oz) butter**
- **1 large tablespoon finely chopped freshly picked parsley**
- **salt & white pepper**
- **lemon juice**

Mix the parsley and butter on a plate with a knife. Add a little white pepper, salt and lemon juice. Leave to set in a cold place.

68. Ham Butter

- **85g (3 oz) butter**
- **110g (4 oz) cooked ham, finely minced**
- **yolk of a hard-boiled egg**
- **1 tablespoon thick cream**
- **natural red colouring**
- **cayenne**

Pound together the finely minced ham, egg yolk, butter and cream. Add a little drop of red colour, and flavour with cayenne. Pass through a sieve or blender. Delicious with chicken or in sandwiches.

69. Grilled Lamb Chops with Victoria Plums

- **4 lamb chops**
- **25 ml red wine vinegar**
- **28g (1 oz) brown sugar**
- **2 tablespoons water**
- **1/4 teaspoon ground cinnamon**
- **8 fresh Victoria plums, halved and stoned**
- **salt and freshly ground black pepper**

Put vinegar, sugar, water and cinnamon in a saucepan and heat until the sugar dissolves. Bring to the boil, add prepared plums, and simmer for about 10 minutes until the plums have softened.
Meanwhile, grill or oven bake the lamb chops until cooked to your liking.
Serve with the sieved plum sauce, along with your favourite potato dish.

70. Sunday Roast Salmon

- **1 whole side of salmon, scaled with skin and bones removed (1350g / 3 lb)**
- **85g (3 oz) butter seasoned with salt, pepper and finely chopped parsley**
- **280 ml (1/2 imperial pint) white wine, water or vinegar**
- **the juice of 2 ripe tomatoes and 2 red capsicums**

Preheat the oven to 400F / 200C / Gas Mark 6. Put the salmon in an oven-proof dish. Combine the rest of the ingredients and pour over the fish. Bake for about 1 hour or until cooked through, basting frequently.
Serve with boiled new potatoes.

71. West Coast Smoked Salmon Surprise
serves 2 for lunch

- **4 slices smoked salmon**
- **4 oz cooked prawns**
- **2 tablespoons mayonnaise**
- **1 tablespoon whipped cream**
- **2 teaspoons tomato purée**
- **1 teaspoon fresh lemon juice**

Mix mayonnaise, cream, tomato purée and lemon juice and fold in prawns. Divide mixture evenly in piles on each salmon slice. Roll salmon slice around prawn mixture and serve with sliced brown wheaten bread, lemon wedges and butter.

72. Devilled Crab

- **1 large crab, boiled**
- **the yolk from 1 hard-boiled egg, rubbed through a sieve**
- **40g (1.5 oz) butter**
- **salt, pepper & cayenne to season**
- **1 large tablespoon cream**
- **1 tablespoon Tartare sauce**
- **a few drops of lemon juice**
- **breadcrumbs**

Remove the meat from the shells and claws of the boiled crab. Clean the shells well and butter the inside of each shell. Shred the crab meat as finely as possible and mix it with the cream, Tartare sauce, 1 tablespoon of breadcrumbs, sieved egg yolk, and 28g (1 oz) of the butter (melted). Season with salt, pepper, lemon juice and a good pinch of cayenne. Mix thoroughly, put in the cleaned crab shells and sprinkle with breadcrumbs. Dot with remaining butter and bake for about 10 minutes until nicely browned.

73. Stewed Stuffed Shoulder of Irish Rosé Veal

- **1 shoulder of Irish Rosé Veal**
- **2 carrots, peeled and left whole**
- **2 onions**
- **a bunch of herbs**
- **28g (1 oz) cornflour**
- **veal stuffing (see following recipe)**

Remove the bone from the shoulder of veal and fill the cavity left by it with veal stuffing. Roll up the veal neatly and tie round firmly with string. Place in a saucepan with just enough water to cover. Add onions, carrots and herbs. Simmer slowly for 3 hours.

To serve, take out the veal, remove the string and strain the gravy into a small saucepan. Bring the gravy to a simmer. Mix the cornflour in a little water and add enough to thicken the gravy according to taste. Chop the vegetables and serve.

74. Veal Stuffing

- **170g (6 oz) breadcrumbs**
- **1 tablespoon finely chopped savoury herbs**
- **85g (3 oz) chopped veal or beef suet**
- **the peel of a lemon, finely chopped**
- **salt and pepper**
- **grated nutmeg**
- **2 eggs**

Beat eggs well and combine with the rest of the ingredients.

Irish Portraits

Josephine & Nellie - the Governess & the Socialite

The Great-Great-Grandmother of Jemima Khan, Theresa Susey Helen Vane-Tempest-Stewart, Marchioness of Londonderry (1856–1919), was known to her friends as Nellie. 'Lady Londonderry was a wonderful woman, with her masculine brain and warm feminine temperament', wrote Lady Fingall. 'The best and staunchest friend in the world, she would back you up through thick and thin.' The novelist and biographer E.F. Benson described Nellie as someone who 'did not plot or plan or devise, she 'went for life' hammer and tongs, she collared it and scragged it and rooked it like a highwaywoman in a tiara'. (Hyde, H.M. p68) Lady Londonderry was a senator of Queen's College Belfast, now known as Queen's University. In 1907 she helped gather up recipes for a fund-raising book to be sold at the Mayflower Stall at Queens College Summer Fête, to raise money for a new athletics field. Miss Josephine Boucher was a governess who lived at 51 Botanic Avenue, close by to Queen's University. Josephine gave Nellie her recipe for Cherry Cakes for inclusion in the fundraising cookbook. Citron can be purchased at most good deli shops; don't mistake it for the rather coarse peel which you find in supermarkets.

75. Cherry Cakes

- 110g (4 oz) butter
- 110g (4 oz) caster sugar
- 170g (6 oz) plain flour
- 28g (1 oz) ground rice
- 3 eggs, at room temperature
- 55g (2 oz) flaked almonds
- 28g (1 oz) whole citron peel, finely chopped
- 55g (2 oz) glace cherries
- vanilla essence
- 1 level teaspoon baking powder

Beat butter and sugar to a cream, then add yolks (not beaten), then vanilla essence. Sieve flour, ground rice and baking powder together, and add alternately with whites of eggs whisked to a froth. Add fruit and flaked almonds. Bake at 180C / 350F / Gas Mark 4 until risen and golden.

The Solicitor

Edward Vicars Hamilton was a well-known solicitor who lived in Omagh at the beginning of the 20th century. He got married, aged 50, around the same time as the Queen's College cookbook was being compiled. His bride was called Marion, and she was 10 years younger than Edward. The Hamiltons contributed their Marrow Marmalade recipe to the Queen's College fundraising book, where it was credited to Mrs. Hamilton, and six years later to Elizabeth Carmichael Ferrall's 'Augher Cookbook' where it was credited to 'Edward. V. Hamilton, ESQ., The Residency, Omagh.'

76. Marrow Marmalade
Edward Vicars Hamilton

- **1.8 kg (4 lb) vegetable marrow**
- **900g (2 lb) apples**
- **2.7 kg (6 lb) sugar**
- **juice and rind of 3 lemons**
- **55g (2 oz) of whole ginger**
- **small teaspoonful of cayenne pepper**
- **1 glass of whiskey**

Slice the marrow, and sprinkle 450g (1 lb) of the sugar on it, and leave overnight. Slice the apples in the same way as you would for a tart. Cut the rind of the lemons as fine as possible, also the ginger, and add these with the remaining sugar to the sliced marrow. Boil all slowly for 2 hours; the syrup should be thick and clear, then add the whiskey and cayenne; allow all to boil for a minute, when it will be done.

The Rector's Daughter, Author's Wife & Hostess

Mrs Florence Elrington Ball, Booterstown House, Co. Dublin (Augher Cookbook)

The daughter of Rev. William Arthur Hamilton DD, rector of Taney, Dundrum, and canon of Christ Church, Dublin, Florence married Dublin author and historian Francis Elrington Ball in 1897. After their marriage their home became a social meeting place in Dublin. The couple had no children and Florence died in 1913, the same year as Elizabeth Carmichael Ferrall published Florence's recipe for fadge in The Augher Cookbook.

F. Elrington Ball's writings contributed considerably to historical records of life in Ireland including 'A history of the county of Dublin: the people, parishes and antiquities from the earliest times to the close of the eighteenth century' which he published in 6 parts from 1902 – 1920.

77. To Make Wheaten Fadge

- **450g (1 lb) wheaten meal**
- **85g (3 oz) butter**
- **1/2 teaspoon salt**
- **1 rounded teaspoon baking powder**
- **1 rounded teaspoon bicarbonate of soda / bread soda**
- **a small cupful of buttermilk, enough to combine to a stiff dough**

Add salt and raising agents to the wheaten meal. Rub in butter finely, then add buttermilk.
Florence wrote... 'The butter well rubbed into the meal. The cakes to be baked slowly on a griddle.'

Turn dough out onto a floured worktop and shape into a round cake. Warm the griddle to a low heat and grease lightly. Mark the dough with a cross. Transfer to the griddle. Cook very slowly, then carefully turn over and bake the other side until cooked through.

Medieval Castle Mistress

Mocollup Castle was a strategic and majestic Irish castle dating from Medieval times. Today, only it's ruins remain. It is located three kilometres west of Ballyduff in Co. Waterford, along the scenic tourist route between Fermoy and Youghal. After the Cromwellian conquest of Ireland the castle was confiscated by the crown and given to Sir Walter Raleigh. He sold it on to the Boyle family (who later became Earls of Cork). The succeeding owner was a Francis Drew (Whelan, A. 2005). The castle was again inhabited in the early 1900s by members of the Drew family relocating from South Africa. Dr. Henry Drew and his wife Cherry were married in 1874 and both they and their ten children, five of whom survived, were all born in South Africa. They retired to the old family property in Ireland bringing their South African cook, Antge van der Berg with them. They also shared their home with several other Irish domestic staff, including local man Patrick Healy, whom they employed as coachman. Cherry Drew contributed the next recipe to Elizabeth Carmichael Ferrall's Augher Cookbook with the recommendation 'Good for children'.

78. An Apple Hedgehog

Bake 3 or 4 **apples** until they feel soft when you pinch them.
Cut **blanched almonds** into 4 (**or** use **flaked almonds**) to form spines.
Place apples close together on a dish, and stick almonds thickly all over the apples. Cover with a **rich sweet custard or whipped cream**.

A Shared Life in Donegal

The internationally acclaimed artist Derek Hill was born in Southampton in 1916. He first worked as a theatre designer in Munich, Paris, Vienna and Sadler's Wells, London and was Head of Art at the British School in Rome during the 1950s. In 1954, at the age of 38, he bought St Columb's in Donegal. The house was built as a rectory in 1828 and had been a fishing hotel for the fifty years before Derek purchased it. It overlooks Gartan Lake, Church Hill, some 10 miles northwest of Letterkenny. Derek loved to travel, and in the same year as he bought his Irish home, he went on a travel trip to Anatolia with the famed explorer and travel writer Dame Freya Stark. Shortly after his return from this trip he employed a housekeeper called Gracie McDermott (née McDaid). Gracie had previously worked in the former hotel as cook, maid and barmaid. She was cook and hostess to his many famous visitors, and treasured friend to Derek for the remaining 35 years of her life.

Amongst Derek's many portraits in galleries around Ireland and Britain is one of Councillor Alban Maginness, Lord Mayor of Belfast 1997 – 1998 which hangs in Belfast City Hall. Many of his works can be viewed on the BBC Your Paintings website. He had a wonderful capacity of expressing the character and spirit of those whom he painted, portraits which included the Irish poet Seamus Heaney and broadcaster Gay Byrne.

In 1981 Derek gifted his home (now open to the public) to the Irish nation along with more than 300 paintings by various 20th century artists, and moved to a small cottage with Gracie. In 1999, the year before he passed away, Derek was made an honorary Irish citizen by President McAleese. She spoke of the tribute to Ireland that such a great artist, who had travelled to some of the most exotic parts of the globe, should have his wanderlust satisfied in Donegal and Tory Island.

Derek rented a small old coastguard hut on Tory Island where he loved to escape and paint the fleeting light changes of the dramatic land and seascapes all around him. In this hut he had a little gas stove on which he liked to cook the following recipe which he named 'Tory Island Cabbage'. Though he loved solitude, he equally loved having the house full of his dearest friends, and his divine tasting St. Patrick's Pudding recipe would have rounded off any banquet in style. No effort was spared in ensuring his guests were indulged and Gracie's Salmon Bisque and homemade Salad Dressing recipe are just a small taste of what it must have been like to dine at the great artist's table. (Recipes by kind permission of Derek's niece Josephine Batterham and PRONI)

79. Tory Island Cabbage

- 1 solid skull shaped white cabbage
- salt & pepper
- béchamel sauce

79b .Béchamel sauce recipe
- 1 best quality chicken stock cube
- 55g (2 oz) butter
- 28g(1 oz) plain flour
- 300 ml scalded milk
- 300 ml boiling water

Dissolve the chicken stock cube in the boiling water. Melt the butter, add the flour and cook out for a few seconds. Gradually add the hot stock and milk. Cook out until thickened, whisking gently all the time.
Stand the cabbage on its side and cut it in slices like you would a loaf of bread. Butter each slice with the béchamel sauce and sprinkle with salt and pepper. Do NOT add cheese as it spoils the taste. Then put the slices back together as though to form a complete cabbage again. Use a tall metal casserole dish which will nicely hold the cabbage in place, and butter it well. Add a dessert-spoon of water to prevent sticking. Set the cabbage in and cover. Put in a very slow oven for up to 3 hours, or on an asbestos mat over a very low gas flame. 'This gives one time to paint and the result is simply delicious'.

80. St. Patrick's Pudding
(As the following dish contains raw egg use pasteurised egg, or eggs from hens which have been vaccinated against salmonella)

- 6 eggs
- 20g (3/4 oz) powdered gelatine
- 3 dessertspoons instant mild powdered coffee
- 3 tablespoons caster sugar
- 135 ml Irish whiskey
- 280 ml (1/2 pint) cream + another 280 ml (1/2 pint) for decoration
- 55g (2 oz) walnuts

Beat the egg yolks, sugar, coffee, gelatine and whiskey over hot water until thick. Remove from heat after a few minutes and place bowl in cold water to cool, beating occasionally until cold. Fold in whipped cream and stiffly beaten egg whites. Turn into a prepared soufflé dish. (Grease base and sides with butter and dust with caster sugar). Put an oiled jam jar in the centre and a fold of greaseproof paper around the dish, bringing it up over the dish to a height of 2.5 cm / 1 inch, to allow to set. Remove paper and jam jar. Fill with whipped cream and decorate with walnuts around edge.

81. Gracie McDermott's Salmon Bisque

- **the head, tail and left over bits of salmon + the rich stock it was cooked in**
- **1 or 2 large onions, chopped**
- **grated nutmeg**
- **paprika**
- **a little powdered tomato to colour**
- **cornflour / cornstarch to thicken**
- **chopped fennel or dill to sprinkle on top**
- **a dollop of cream (optional)**
- **croutons or diced cucumber softened in milk**

Simmer the leftover salmon and stock with the onion and a little grated nutmeg. Sieve and put good remains back into the liquid. Add paprika and powdered tomato for taste and colour and thicken with a little cornflour which has been dissolved in cold water. Serve with a dollop of cream if liked, a sprinkle of chopped herbs, and croutons or diced cucumber which has been softened in milk.

82. Gracie's Salad Dressing

- **1 cup of vinegar**
- **1 cup of oil**
- **two and a half tablespoons sugar**
- **1 egg**

Mix vinegar, sugar and oil and boil for 5 minutes. Cool. Add beaten egg and bring just to simmering point. Cool. Store in jars.

The Nurse and Friend of Florence Nightingale

The next recipe was submitted to the Queens College recipe book by a close friend of Florence Nightingale. Ada Bourne grew up on the family farm in Staffordshire and was a ward sister in St. Thomas' hospital. She married Sir William Whitla, a native of County Monaghan, and became known as Lady Whitla. Sir William Whitla was physician to Belfast Royal Hospital from 1882 to 1918. The Whitlas had no children and travelled extensively, visiting Russia, Canada and many Mediterranean cities. Sir William Whitla was also a prolific writer with many of his works being translated into other languages, including Chinese. Lady Whitla was deeply religious, and a member of The Salvation Army. On the occasion of her husband's knighthood, Lady Whitla wore her Salvation Army uniform to Buckingham Palace, a strong contrast to the lascivious lifestyle of the wealthy at that time, and was said by many to be an implied reprimand to the reigning playboy King Edward VII. William Whitla bequeathed his home at Lennoxvale as an official residence for the Vice Chancellor of Queen's University. The Whitla Medical Building and Whitla Hall stand today as a testament to the generosity of this philanthropic couple.

83. Vinegar Pastry (A very old recipe)
Lady Whitla

- **225g (8 oz) plain flour**
- **1 egg**
- **225g (8 oz) butter**
- **30 ml (2 x 15 ml tablespoons) white vinegar**

Rub the butter into the flour well. Beat the egg, then mix well with the vinegar, then add to the flour mixture. Handle it as little as possible. Set aside for 2 hours; roll out in very thin layers, and bake in a hot oven.

The Donegal Hotel Proprietress

Prospect Hotel was situated on the seafront in Moville on the beautiful Inishowen peninsula in Donegal. Unfortunately the premises burnt down recently and have not been rebuilt. The hotel was originally run by Hannah Beatty and her daughter Lily. Lily wrote down all her recipes meticulously; even going so far as to number them and write her own index. The next 8 recipes are from that very notebook. The notebook dates pre and during the First World War years. (Recipes by kind permission of Lily's daughter Bettine Simpson and granddaughter Pat Hey).

84. Spiced Beef

- **225g (1/2 lb) salt**
- **225g (1/2 lb) sugar**
- **2 slightly rounded teaspoons (1/2 oz) salt petre**
- **2 slightly rounded teaspoons (1/2 oz) pepper**
- **2 slightly rounded teaspoons (1/2 oz) allspice**
- **1 teaspoon ground mace**
- **1 teaspoon ground cinnamon**
- **3.1 kg (7 lbs) rump of beef**

Mix first 7 ingredients in a crock, set in the meat and rub the salt and spices mixture into it. Turn and rub every day for 10 days or longer. Wash spices off and steam for two hours. To steam - put a little water in a saucepan, with a close fitting lid, when boiling put in meat and turn often.

85. Brown Sauce

- 1 teaspoon sugar
- 1 teaspoon vinegar
- 28g (1 oz) butter
- 28g (1 oz) 1 rasher bacon or rinds
- 28g (1 oz) plain all purpose flour
- 560 ml (1 pint) of stock or water
- seasonings
- pieces of carrot, onion and celery
- 1 tomato
- 4 or 5 cloves
- piece of cinnamon
- blade of mace
- 1/2 teaspoon mixed herbs

Put sugar in a stew pan and let it get brown. Add vinegar and let it vaporise, put in butter and bacon next and brown it, then add in all the vegetables and herbs. Fry until they are browned, stirring all the time. Put flour in to absorb grease, add the liquid and stir until it boils. Season to taste. Boil awhile, strain and serve. This sauce keeps a fortnight by boiling it occasionally.

86. Rhubarb or Gooseberry Chutney

- 900g (2 lb) rhubarb or gooseberries
- 900g (2 lb) sultanas
- 900g (2 lb) sugar
- 28 g (1 oz) garlic, cut very fine
- 28g (1 oz) salt
- 28g (1 oz) ground ginger
- 560 ml (1 pint) vinegar
- 6 chillies
- 1 small bottle Worcestershire sauce

Wash fruit (if using rhubarb, cut it up).
Skin lemons and cut up pulp finely.
Chop garlic very fine.
Put all into an enamelled saucepan to boil until it becomes thick.
Put into jars. It is better if kept for two years before using.

87. Parsley Honey

- 140g (5 oz) parsley
- 840 ml (1.5 pints) water
- 450g (1 lb) sugar
- 1 teaspoon vinegar
- a little lemon
- flavouring

Boil the parsley in the water until liquid is reduced to 560 ml (1 pint). Strain off the parsley and boil the sugar and water and flavourings till the mixture thickens.

88. Turnip au Gratin

Pare **turnips** finely and cut into slices. Lay slices in a well-**butter**ed baking dish. Pour over 280 ml (1/2 Imperial pint) of **nice white sauce**, and sprinkle with **grated cheese** and **fine breadcrumbs**. Dot with tiny lumps of butter. Cover and bake in the oven until turnips are quite tender; if the turnips are at all frost-bitten, it is wise to parboil them at first.

89. Rissoles

- 335g (3/4 lb) cold cooked meat
- 28g (1 oz) butter
- 28g (1 oz) plain flour
- 1 teacupful breadcrumbs or mashed potatoes
- 1 tablespoon chopped onion
- 1 teacup milk or stock
- some parsley or dried herbs
- seasoning
- 1 dessertspoon sauce or relish

Mince the meat and mix it with the onion, herbs, relish, breadcrumbs or potatoes and seasoning. Melt butter, add flour and mix into a stiff sauce with the milk or stock. Pour into the meat mixture and mix well. Add a little egg to bind it. Make into cork shaped pieces, brush with beaten egg and coat with very fine breadcrumbs. Fry in smoking fat until brown. Dry on kitchen paper, serve on fancy doily with parsley as a garnish.

90. Urney Pudding
From the district of Urney, Strabane, County Tyrone.

- 2 eggs
- 110g (1/4 lb) butter
- 110g (1/4 lb) plain flour, sieved
- 55g (2 oz) sugar
- 1 tablespoon raspberry jam
- 1 level teaspoon baking powder

Grease a pudding bowl and sugar it. Put butter and sugar into a basin and beat until creamy. Mix in the baking powder, eggs, flour and jam. Put into mould or pudding basin and cover with greased paper. Cover with a double layer of kitchen foil and tie securely in place. Set the pudding in a steamer (or on an upturned plate in a saucepan) and steam over (or in) a pan of boiling water for about 2 hours. (top up the water as needed to ensure the pan does not boil dry). Turn out and serve with custard sauce.

91. Ginger Wine

- **450g (1 lb) sugar**
- **2.24 litres (4 pints) hot water**
- **2 dessertspoons essence of ginger**
- **2 dessertspoons essence of Cayenne**
- **2 dessertspoons essence of lemon**
- **28g (1 oz) burnt sugar**
- **14g (1/2 oz) tartaric acid**
- **½ wineglass rum or whiskey in each bottle**

Dissolve sugar in the hot water, add next 5 ingredients, bottle with 1/2 wineglass rum or whiskey in each bottle.

The County Fermanagh Shopkeeper

Sarah Flynn's Grocer and General Merchant's store was just past the bridge as you leave the little riverside village of Kesh, heading for Belleek and Donegal. (Recipes by kind permission of Sarah Flynn's family)

92. Baked Salmon Trout

- **1 large salmon trout**

Fish Forcemeat Stuffing
- **28g (1 oz) fine stale bread crumbs**
- **60 ml milk**
- **1 egg, well beaten**
- **85g (3 oz) raw fish**
- **salt**

Cook bread and milk to a paste, add beaten egg and fish pounded and forced through a puree strainer. Season with salt.

Prepare cooking sauce for trout:
- **280 ml (1/2 pint) water**
- **280 ml (1/2 pint) vinegar**
- **a good piece of butter**
- **a little chopped carrot**
- **onion**
- **6 peppercorns**
- **1 bayleaf**
- **1 clove**
- **1 sprig of thyme**
- **basil**
- **1 tablespoon of chopped parsley**
- **a good pinch of salt**

Boil all for 3 minutes. Strain.

When fish is cooked you will need,
- **28g (1 oz) butter**
- **28g (1 oz) plain flour**
- **a little cream**
- **a drop or 2 of anchovy /fish sauce**
- **salt and pepper to taste**

Stuff the trout with the fish forcemeat and fix its tail in its mouth. Put it into a buttered earthenware dish and cover it with the strained sauce. Bake in the oven. Baste with the sauce from time to time as the fish is cooking. When the fish is cooked, strain the sauce. Melt 28g (1 oz) butter in a saucepan, mix in 28g (1 oz) of plain flour, cook out a little then add the strained liquid. Simmer to a smooth sauce, whisking all the time, and add a little cream, anchovy / fish sauce, salt and pepper to taste. Finally, just before serving, add a little butter the size of a walnut to give the sauce a gloss. Serve sauce in a sauce boat.

93. *Buttermilk Brack*

- **225g (8 oz) plain flour**
- **110g (4 oz) margarine**
- **140g (5 oz) caster sugar**
- **225g (8 oz) mixed fruit**
- **2 small eggs**
- **1/2 rounded teaspoon bicarbonate of soda / bread soda**
- **1/4 teaspoon mixed spice**
- **1/4 teaspoon cinnamon**
- **buttermilk to mix**

Rub margarine into flour, add the other ingredients. Mix to a firm consistency with beaten eggs and buttermilk. Bake at 180C / 350F / Gas Mark 4 until golden brown. Serve buttered slices for tea or supper.

94. *Ivory Cream Recipe*

- 470 ml rich milk
- 170g (6 oz) sugar
- 1.5 tablespoons gelatine
- 60 ml cold water
- 1 teaspoon vanilla
- 120 ml cream or evaporated milk, whipped
- more cream to serve

Soak gelatine for 5 minutes in cold water. Heat milk in a double boiler with sugar and gelatine. When scalded, cool and add vanilla. As it begins to thicken, stir in whipped cream, pour into a mould and chill until set. Unmould and serve with sliced peaches or seasonal berries, and whipped cream.

The Private Secretary

From Jenny McKee's handwritten City and Guilds Cookery Notebook 1914-1915

Jenny McKee, from Tynan in County Armagh, was private secretary to Hugh MacDowell Pollock, Northern Ireland's first Finance Minister 1921 - 1937. (Recipes by kind permission of Dorothy Bruce)

95. Brown Soda Bread

- **225g (1/2 lb) wholemeal flour - oaten or barley meal may also be used**
- **225 g (1/2 lb) plain flour**
- **1/2 teaspoon salt**
- **1 level teaspoon bicarbonate of soda / bread soda**
- **1 level teaspoon cream of tartar**
- **28g (1 oz) margarine**
- **buttermilk to mix**

Mix the dry ingredients together and rub in the margarine to resemble fine breadcrumbs. Gradually add sufficient buttermilk to mix to a light, elastic dough. Turn the bread onto a lightly floured board, roll out thinly and evenly, cut into four, cook slowly on the griddle, first on one side, then turn and cook on second side. If the bread is wished rough looking, use wheaten meal instead of flour on the baking board.

96. Potato Pastry

This pastry is an economical one and may be used in the same way as short pastry. It makes beautiful pastry for an apple cake.

- **110g (4 oz) plain flour**
- **110g (4 oz) mashed potatoes**
- **pinch of salt**
- **55 – 85 g (2 -3 oz) margarine**
- **1 teaspoon baking powder**
- **cold water to mix**

Rub the margarine into the flour, add other ingredients, mix to a rolling consistency with water. Use as required.

97. Tuesday's Pudding

On 15 June 1914 Grant Richards published the first edition of James Joyce's Dubliners. The narrative accounts give us an interesting insight into everyday Dublin life at that time. Joyce's short story 'The Boarding House' shows just how little was wasted in Irish kitchens of the past.

'Mrs. Mooney sat in the straw arm-chair and watched the servant Mary remove the breakfast things. She made Mary collect the crusts and pieces of broken bread to help to make Tuesday's bread-pudding.'

Coincidentally Jenny McKee handwrote this popular Irish pudding recipe in her student notebook on Tuesday 1st December 1914.

Steamed Scrap Bread Pudding

- **225g (1/2 lb) scraps of bread**
- **55g (2 oz) suet**
- **28g (1 oz) plain flour**
- **28g (1 oz) raisins**
- **55g (2 oz) sugar**
- **55g (2 oz) currants**
- **pinch of salt**
- **½ teaspoon mixed spice**
- **¼ teaspoon bicarbonate of soda /bread soda**
- **buttermilk to mix**

Soak the bread in cold water for 1 hour, or overnight if necessary. Drain away the water and wring the bread through a clean tea cloth until it is as dry as possible. Crumb the bread lightly with a fork. Add the prepared fruit, the chopped suet, and all the dry ingredients. Mix thoroughly and add buttermilk to moisten. Turn into a prepared bowl, cover with buttered paper and steam for two and a half hours.

98. Sherry – makes 6 fine noggin bottles

This recipe was handwritten on a loose page and tucked inside Jenny's 1914 – 1915 class notebook.

- **4.5 litres (1 gallon) lukewarm water**
- **1350g (3 lb) sugar**
- **900g (2 lb) raisins**
- **14g (1/2 oz) yeast**
- **3 potatoes (finely chopped)**

Put everything into a crock or enamel pot big enough to leave room to stir. Leave for 3 weeks, stirring every day. Strain and bottle. (Put 1 tablespoon of brown sugar at the bottom of each bottle to collect sediment). Leave corks loose for 10 days after bottling.

99. Sponge Cake

A dry sponge, perfect for a flan case or trifle sponges.

- **3 eggs**
- **85g (3 oz) caster sugar**
- **85g (3 oz) plain flour**

Preheat the oven to 325F / 170C /gas Mark 3. Grease and line a flan or swiss roll tin. Weigh out the flour, sieve it and set aside.
Place the eggs and the sugar into a mixing basin and whisk over hot water until thick and white.
Very lightly stir in the sieved flour, turn into prepared tin, and bake at a steady, very moderate heat for 40 – 50 minutes.

King Cormac, The High King of Ireland
(from the ancient Triads of Ireland, circa 500 AD)

A Recipe for Success

'Be not too wise, be not too foolish,
be not too conceited, nor too diffident,
be not too haughty, nor too humble,
be not too talkative, nor too silent,
be not too hard, nor too feeble,
If you be too wise, one will expect too much of you;
If you be foolish, you will be deceived;
If you be too conceited, you will be thought vexatious;
If you be too humble, you will be without honour;
If you be too talkative, you will not be heeded;
If you be too silent, you will not be regarded;
If you be too hard, you will be broken;
If you be too feeble, you will be crushed.'

Sweet Bakes

100. Belfast Florence Cake

Florence cake has been traditionally baked in Northern Ireland by the larger commercial bakeries for many decades, and nearly every household seems to buy one on a regular basis. It comes in a traditional baker's cardboard box with a clear window, and is simply a sort of round Madeira cake covered in white icing with a cherry in the middle. My sons prefer our homemade version and make short work of this every time. We usually ice ours a light shade of blue. A really useful quick standby recipe to call on – just keep some cream cheese handy in the fridge. You can bake 2 cakes to make a large birthday cake. Just sandwich together with buttercream and cover with ready rolled icing.

- 140g (5 oz) butter or soft margarine
- 140g (5 oz) cream cheese
- 225g (8 oz) caster sugar
- 3 medium eggs, at room temperature
- 170g (6 oz) self-raising flour, sieved
- 2 teaspoons vanilla essence
- icing to cover + 1 glacé cherry to top

Preheat oven to 170C / 325 F / Gas Mark 3. Grease and line a round cake tin (20 cm in diameter, 5 cm deep / 8inch by 2 inch).
Cream the butter or margarine with the sugar and soft cheese and vanilla essence. Add eggs one at a time, beating well as you add each one. Fold in sieved flour.
Bake for 30 – 45 minutes until risen and baked through to centre.
Decorate with fondant icing and a cherry atop.

101. Date 'n' Walnut Cake

- 55g (2oz) butter or margarine, at room temperature
- 110 g (4 oz) brown sugar
- 1 large egg, at room temperature, well beaten
- 110g (4 oz) plain flour
- 55g (2oz) chopped walnuts + a few extra for decoration
- 225g (8 oz) chopped dates
- 1/2 rounded teaspoon bicarbonate of soda / bread soda
- 6oml lukewarm water
- 1/2 teaspoon vanilla essence
- 1/4 teaspoon salt

Line a 450g /1 lb / 16 x 11 x 7cm loaf tin with baking paper.
Preheat oven to 275F/ 140 C/ Gas Mark 1.
Cream butter and sugar and add well beaten egg. Sieve the flour and salt together. Dissolve bicarbonate of soda and vanilla in the water. Add flour and water mixture alternately to the creamed mixture in steps until all is combined. Stir in the chopped dates and walnuts.
Bake slowly until risen and cooked through.

102. Kerry Apple Cake

- 225g (8 oz) plain flour
- 110g (4 oz) butter or margarine
- 1 egg
- 335 g (3/4 lb) apples
- 140g (5 oz) caster sugar
- 1 rounded teaspoon baking powder
- a little milk

Grease and line a Swiss roll tin and pre-heat oven to 400°F / 200°C /Gas Mark 6. Rub butter into flour. Add sugar and baking powder. Peel and chop apples. Add them to flour with beaten egg and enough milk to moisten into a stiff dough. Put into Swiss roll tin and bake for 20 to 30 minutes.

103. Irish Porter Cake

Irish Porter Cake is a large fruit cake which often takes pride of place at family gatherings and even in some traditional Irish pubs. This recipe makes 2 cakes in 900g / 1 lb loaf tins, though you could bake all in one large traditional round tin; it will just take longer to cook.

Let your cakes cool for 6 hours before wrapping in tin foil to mature for a few days. It takes about 6 hours for the cakes inner core temperature to cool completely. This is the reason my Grandmother cooled food by the window or even outside, sometimes wrapped in tea towels and set high up in the branches of a tree. The faster you can cool the core temperature, the better your cake will keep.

- 225g (8oz) sunflower margarine
- 225g (8 oz) Demerara sugar
- 280ml (1/2 pint) black stout
- 800g / 1 lb 12 oz) mixed dried fruit
- 425g / (15 oz) plain flour
- 85g (3 oz) strong white bread flour
- 1 rounded teaspoon baking powder
- 1/2 rounded teaspoon bicarbonate of soda / bread soda
- 1 level teaspoon ground cinnamon
- 1/2 level teaspoon ground cloves
- 1/2 level teaspoon freshly grated nutmeg
- 1.5 level teaspoons ground ginger
- 1/2 level teaspoon ground allspice
- 3 large or 4 small eggs

Grease and line 2 x 900g / 2 lb loaf tins. Preheat oven to 170 C / 325F / Gas Mark 3.

Melt margarine, sugar, stout and fruit in saucepan together. When margarine is fully melted and heated through, remove from heat. Leave to cool until it is not too hot to touch.

Mix flours, spices and raising agents together in a bowl.

Add partly cooled fruit mixture and quickly mix together. Add eggs and mix quickly again. Pour into tins and bake for 1 hr 15 minutes, (reducing heat to 150 C /300 F / Gas Mark 2 after the first half hour) until baked through. Increase oven time if making one large cake.

104. Simple Irish Baker's Short Paste

Use this to line little individual tarts, pastry based traybakes, or even to knock up a quick fruit pie. With this recipe you should never feel the need to buy readymade shortcrust pastry again.

- **225 g (8 oz) plain flour**
- **110 g (4 oz) butter or margarine**
- **85 g (3 oz) caster sugar**
- **1 egg**

Rub or cut in the margarine into the flour until it resembles fine breadcrumbs. In a separate bowl mix the egg with the sugar to form a paste. Add this paste to the flour and mix together to form a dough. Do not overmix.

Roll out on a well floured worktop, sprinkling with a little more flour as needed. This is a soft shortpaste which only requires gentle handling for superb, speedy results.

105. Blackcurrant & Bramley Apple Tart

- **1 large Bramley apple (about 225g / 1/2 lb in weight)**
- **410g (14.5 oz) can blackcurrant fruit filling**
- **sugar to taste**
- **225 g (8 oz) plain flour**
- **110 g (4 oz) butter or margarine**
- **85 g (3 oz) caster sugar**
- **1 egg**

Use a 9 inch / 23 cm tart plate. Preheat oven to 325°F/ 170°C / Gas Mark 3. Rub margarine into flour finely to resemble fine breadcrumbs. Mix egg with caster sugar to form a paste. Combine this with the flour to form a soft dough. Flour worktop well. Roll out one larger circle for the base and a slightly smaller circle for the top. This pastry is very soft; use a rolling pin to roll up and lay out across dish. Don't worry if it splits; the pastry is easily patched anywhere it needs it. Thinly slice apple and lay across pastry base. Sprinkle with sugar to taste. Cover with a layer of blackcurrant fruit filling, and top with pastry lid. Mark a cross in the middle of pastry as a vent to let air out, prick several times across the top with a fork, and bake slowly for about one hour until golden. Sprinkle with sugar when baked.

106. Irish Plate Apple Tart (really thin pastry)

This quantity makes enough for a large 27 cm / 11 inch diameter deep apple tart with some pastry left for a few individual little pies; or you could make 2 medium sized pies, whichever you fancy!

- **450g (1 lb) plain flour**
- **1/2 rounded teaspoon baking powder**
- **1/4 level teaspoon salt**
- **225g (1/2 lb) lard**
- **1 small egg**
- **20 ml (4 teaspoons) white vinegar**
- **85 ml water**
- **14g (1/2 oz) sugar**
- **whipped egg white + caster sugar to sprinkle on top**
- **Bramley cooking apples**
- **sugar to sweeten apples according to taste**

Grease a pie plate generously. Put all dry ingredients in a bowl and mix well. Cut fat up into small pieces and rub into flour till it resembles fine bread-crumbs. In a separate bowl blend egg, vinegar and water together. Add this to mixing bowl and bind together. Do not over mix. If very dry add a tiny bit more water. Work quickly with this pastry as it much easier to roll with when it is just made. Set out on a well-floured worktop and divide in two.
Roll out first piece quite thinly to line base and sides of pie dish. Fill with freshly sliced Bramley apples, adding sugar to sweeten. Roll out lid larger than size needed and lay pastry over the top of the pie. Gently push down around edge of pie dish to form crust and cut off excess pastry with a knife. Glaze pastry lid of pie with beaten egg white and sprinkle caster sugar on top. Set on a tray lined with greaseproof to catch any leakage of fruit.
Bake at 170C / 325F/ Gas Mark 3 for around an hour, or until well browned.

107. Apple Tart (thick pastry)

Pastry:
- **335g (12 oz) plain flour**
- **55g (2 oz) caster sugar**
- **½ rounded teaspoon bicarbonate of soda / bread soda**
- **pinch of salt**
- **85g (3 oz) butter**
- **142 ml buttermilk**
- **1 large egg**

Filling:
- **675g (1.5 lb) Irish Bramley cooking apples (weight before peeling)**
- **110g -170g (4 - 6 oz) caster sugar**

Bake as a round pie or use a deep Swiss roll tin to make into apple squares. If using ordinary sweet apples cut the sugar amount given for the filling.
Sieve the flour, salt, bicarbonate of soda and sugar into a bowl. Chop the butter into small pieces and rub into the flour mixture until all resembles fine breadcrumbs. Whisk the egg, mix with the buttermilk, and add this to the rest of the ingredients in the bowl. Mix to a soft dough and turn out onto a well-floured worktop. Divide mixture in two, and roll out first piece into a round or rectangle, depending on shape of dish or tray used. Grease dish or tin generously and line with pastry. Preheat the oven to 180C / 350F /Gas Mark 4. Peel the apples and slice them over the pastry base, adding as much sugar as necessary to sweeten them. Roll out the second piece of pastry to form a lid. Seal the edges and prick all over with a fork to allow steam to escape. Sprinkle a little sugar over the top of the pie. Put a lined tray on the shelf below pie to catch any syrup which may bubble out during baking. Bake in the oven for 30 – 45 minutes. If baked in a rectangular or square tin, cut into squares or fingers while still hot. Sprinkle a little more sugar over the top if you wish.

108. Irish Boiled Fruit Cake

The Irish solution to traditional dry fruit cakes. Although the title sound a little strange to the uninitiated, a boiled fruit cake is actually one of the nicest fruit cakes you can make. The rehydration of the fruit makes the cake wonderfully moist, and the spices mature and taste even better after a few days sitting in a tin in a cool part of your kitchen. The cake is baked, not boiled as the title would seem to suggest. Try spreading slices with a little butter, the traditional way to serve this Irish fruit cake.

- **310g (11 oz) sultanas**
- **110g (4 oz) sugar**
- **110g (4 oz) butter**
- **60 ml water**
- **60 ml sherry**
- **1 x 5ml teaspoon browning (for cakes and puddings)**

Combine the above ingredients and leave to steep for an hour or two, or overnight. When steeped, bring to a simmer on a medium heat and when the butter has melted, leave aside to cool to hand heat. Preheat oven to 325F / 170C / Gas Mark 3.
Meanwhile weigh out the following and sieve together:

- **85g (3 oz) self-raising flour**
- **55g (2 oz) plain flour**
- **28g (1 oz) extra strong bread flour**
- **1/4 teaspoon ground allspice**
- **1/4teaspoon ground cinnamon**
- **1/2 teaspoon ground ginger**
- **1 level teaspoon mixed spice**
- **1/4 teaspoon ground cloves**
- **1/3 teaspoon bicarbonate of soda / bread soda**

Grease and line a 23 x 13 x 7cm / 2 lb loaf tin.
Gently whisk 2 medium sized eggs and set aside.
Add cooled fruit mixture to the dry ingredients. Mix quickly and add whisked eggs stirring together until combined. Transfer mixture quickly to lined tin and place in preheated oven. Bake for about an hour, or until a skewer inserted into centre of cake comes out clean.
Allow to cool on a wire tray for 6 hours before storing in an airtight tin in a cool place.

109. Pineapple Boiled Fruit Cake

- **225g (8 oz) self-raising flour**
- **2 eggs at room temperature**
- **170g (6 oz) soft brown sugar**
- **110g (4 oz) butter or margarine**
- **225g (8 oz) small tin of crushed pineapple including juice**
- **280g (10 oz) mixed dried fruit**
- **110g (4 oz) glace cherries, chopped**

Grease and line a 900g / 2 lb loaf tin.
Put sugar, butter, crushed pineapple and its juice, mixed fruit and cherries into a saucepan. Bring to the boil, then simmer gently for about 5 minutes. Remove from heat and leave to cool down for about 20 minutes.
Preheat oven to 325 F/ 170 C / Gas Mark 3.
When mixture has cooled, add self-raising flour and eggs and mix together until combined. Transfer to lined tin and bake in centre of oven for about an hour until cooked through to centre. The cake is ready when risen and a skewer inserted into the centre comes away clean.

110. Gluten Free Yogurt Cake

- **1 x 125g (4.5 oz) carton yogurt – use any flavour yogurt**
- **1 same carton full of sunflower oil**
- **2 cartons caster sugar**
- **3 cartons self-raising gluten free flour**
- **4 eggs, lightly beaten**
- **1 or 2 teaspoons flavouring essence according to taste and yogurt used**

Preheat oven to 180 C / 350 F / Gas Mark 4.
Line a 900g / 2 lb tin.
Put all ingredients in a bowl and mix together.
Transfer to tin and bake for approximately 45 minutes.

111. Rose Fondant Icing

- **fondant icing sugar**
- **natural red colouring**
- **a little rose-water**

Make up fondant icing according to packet instructions, substituting a little of water used with rose-water, and adding a few drops of colouring to obtain a rose pink colour.

112. Chocolate Cake

- **225g (8oz) plain flour, sieved**
- **225g (8 oz) butter or margarine**
- **225g (8 oz) caster sugar, sieved**
- **225g (8 oz) milk chocolate, grated, then melted**
- **110g (4 oz) ground almonds**
- **7 eggs at room temperature**
- **1 heaped teaspoon of Sal Volatile (baking powder)**

Grease and line a 23cm x 7 cm / 9 inch spring form cake tin. Beat the butter or margarine to a cream. Beat the yolks of 7 eggs into this, and beat in the melted, grated chocolate. Add the sieved flour and the sieved sugar, ground almonds and raising agent. Beat up the whites of the eggs to form stiff peaks and add them.
Bake in a slow oven 300-325F / 150-160C / Gas Mark 2 - 3 for 1 – 1.5 hours or until baked through. Remove from tin and set on a cooling rack.

112b. Chocolate Icing

- **85g (3 oz) milk chocolate**
- **60 ml boiling water**
- **170g (6 oz) sieved icing sugar**

Grate milk chocolate into boiling water.
Mix well until melted then set aside to cool.
When it has cooled gradually add sieved icing sugar. When the right consistency to coat the back of a wooden spoon is reached, pour over cake.

113. Seed Cake with Almonds

- 110g (4 oz) butter
- 110g (4 oz) caster sugar
- 2 large eggs, beaten
- 140g (5 oz) self-raising flour
- 28g (1 oz) ground almonds
- enough milk to make a dropping consistency
- 2 rounded teaspoons caraway seeds

Topping:-
- 2 tablespoons Demerara sugar
- 1 tablespoon flaked almonds

Preheat oven to 325 F / 170 C /Gas Mark 4. Grease and line a 17.5 cm / 7 inch round cake tin. Cream butter and caster sugar well together. Mix in the ground almonds. Beat in the eggs. Fold in the caraway seeds and flour. Add a few tablespoons of milk to make a dropping consistency. Fill the mixture into the tin and level it over. Sprinkle Demerara sugar over the top, then the flaked almonds. Bake in preheated oven for around an hour, or until a skewer inserted in centre comes out clean.

114. Bramley Apple Gingerbread

- 225g (1/2 lb) Bramley cooking apples
- 85g (3 oz) Demerara sugar
- 110g (4 oz) golden syrup
- 85g (3 oz) butter
- 170g (6 oz) self-raising flour
- 1 rounded teaspoon ground ginger
- 1/4 teaspoon ground cloves
- 1 egg

Peel and slice the apples. Put apples in a saucepan with 1 dessertspoonful of sugar and just enough water to keep from burning. Stew until soft, mash and leave to cool. Put syrup, butter and the rest of the sugar in saucepan, dissolve slowly and set aside to cool also. Whisk egg well, add cooled syrup mixture, and combine. Gently add sieved flour, ginger and cloves, then fold in apple and combine all together well. Put in a greased and lined tin and bake in a moderate oven, 325F / 170C / Gas Mark 3 for about half an hour.

115. Botanic Apple Cheesecakes

- **Some ready-made puff pastry**
- **225g (1/2 lb) apple pulp**
- **110g (1/4 lb) sieved sugar**
- **110g (1/4 lb) butter, melted and cooled slightly**
- **4 eggs, separated**
- **finely grated rind and juice of 1 lemon**

Pare, core and boil sufficient apples to make ½ lb when cooked, or use ready-made apple purée. Whisk half of the egg whites (the remainder of the whites are not required for this recipe). Lightly whisk all of the egg yolks, and add these, together with the sugar, whisked egg whites, butter and lemon rind and juice, to the apple purée. Stir mixture well. Line some patty tins with puff pastry, add spoonfuls of apple mixture, and bake for about 20 minutes in a moderate oven. Makes 18 to 20 cheesecakes

116. Coconut Macaroon Tartlets

- **small batch of shortcrust pastry**
- **seedless mixed fruit or raspberry jam**
- **4 medium to large egg whites at room temperature**
- **280g (10 oz) caster sugar**
- **140g (5 oz) extra fine dessicated coconut**
- **28g (1 oz) ground rice**

Make individual pastry cases with the shortcrust pastry, (don't roll out pastry too thickly) and line small bun tins with circles of pastry to form pastry cases. Pipe approximately 1 heaped teaspoonful of jam across base of each pastry case.

Make the topping - Put egg whites and caster sugar in a spotlessly clean (oil free) bowl and whisk until they form very high peaks. Meanwhile mix the coconut and ground rice together by hand, making sure there are no lumps. When egg whites are ready add coconut and rice carefully by hand, taking only a few seconds to mix so as not to collapse the meringue. Pipe into the prepared pastry and jam cases. Bake at 325F/ 170C / gas Mark 3 for 30 -45 minutes, or until meringue does not break when you tap it gently.

117. Pineapple Creams

One of the top-selling pastries in home bakery shops across Northern Ireland are Pineapple Creams. Sweet short paste shells, a little crushed or chopped pineapple on the base, topped with not too sweet synthetic cream, and decorated with yellow pineapple flavoured fondant – they are harder to find than they used to be, since many family run bakeries have vanished from the high streets. Pineapple Creams are pretty easy to make if you substitute the mock cream filling with sweetened fresh double cream, and use sweetened chopped fresh pineapple. The recent availability of fondant icing sugar in the supermarkets makes the fondant icing easier than ever to replicate at home.

For the pastry shells:
- **110g (4 oz) plain flour**
- **55g (2oz) butter**
- **1 egg yolk**
- **28g (1 oz) caster sugar**

Preheat oven to 325F / 170 C / Gas Mark 3.
Rub the butter into the flour until the mixture resembles fine breadcrumbs. Combine the egg yolk with the caster sugar to form a paste and add to the breadcrumb mixture.
Mix together lightly until a dough is formed. If the mixture is too stiff to form a dough add a drop or two of water, but don't let the dough get sticky. Roll out on a floured worktop. Using a large biscuit cutter, glass or mug, stamp out circles a little larger than the cases you are going to line. Carefully set the pastry circles inside silver mince pie cases or muffin tins. Now using the same cutter, mark out circles of greaseproof silicone paper and cut these out.
Gently set paper circles on top of the pastry and hold down with dried peas or rice. Bake in the preheated oven until a light golden colour.

Filling:
- **small tin of crushed pineapple, or fresh pineapple**
- **250 ml fresh double cream**
- **sieved icing sugar to sweeten cream**
- **vanilla essence**

Set enough chopped, tinned or fresh pineapple to cover bases of pastry in a sieve, and leave to drain into a bowl.
When drained well, set a small amount of pineapple into the base of each pastry shell.

Beat cream, and fold in some sieved icing sugar and a few drops of vanilla essence to taste. Divide whipped double cream evenly over each pastry shell and smooth out.

Pineapple Fondant Topping:

- • 250 g (9 oz) fondant icing sugar
- • a few teaspoons pineapple juice
- • yellow food colouring

Sieve the fondant icing sugar into a bowl.
Add pineapple juice, a teaspoon full at a time, and mix to icing consistency.
Add a few drops of yellow food colouring until desired colour is reached.
Spoon or pipe over the top of the pineapple and cream filled pastry shells.
Leave to set in the fridge.

118. Irish Rock Buns

Even though these are called Rock Buns, they are more a cross between a scone and a bun, and great anytime with a cup of tea. If the cherries are especially syrupy and broken this recipe comes out even better, as the cherries disperse through the bun giving it a pinkish tinge and a lovely flavour. This is the recipe I used to make in Mum's kitchen when I was 12. There was just enough time to leg it to Wellworths supermarket to stock up on ingredients before I caught the Ulsterbus home after school each day. Laden down with bags of flour, eggs and cherries, I was counting those pennies and pounds I would exchange my freshly baked rock buns for when Dad had sold them to regular weekly customers across County Fermanagh.

- 55g (2 oz) strong bread flour
- 390g (14 oz) self-raising flour
- 170g (6 oz) sultanas
- 225g (8 oz) glace cherries
- 225g (8 oz) margarine
- 170g (6 oz) caster sugar + a little extra to sprinkle on baked rock buns
- 2 eggs
- a little milk to bind

Rub margarine into sugar and flours. Add sultanas and chopped cherries. Add blended eggs and milk to bind. If needed add a little extra milk to form a stiff dough. Put in rocky mounds on a baking tray lined with silicone paper, leaving room between for dough flattening out during baking. Bake at 350F/180C/ Gas Mark 4 till golden. Do not overbake. Sprinkle with caster sugar when baked.

119. Mum's easy 3,4,5,6 Buns

Named thanks to their easy to remember formula using old Imperial ounce measurements; it was easy to rhyme off - three of eggs, four of margarine, five of sugar and six of flour; before you knew it, these wee buns were in and out of the oven in a flash. Perfect when you're in a hurry, this recipe tastes best eaten the day it is made. It can also be used to make a beautiful coffee, coconut or chocolate sandwich cake (lower temperature by one setting as the cake will take a little longer to cook through), and tastes great iced with flavoured light buttercream and chocolate flakes or walnuts.

- **3 eggs, at room temperature**
- **110 g / 4oz soft margarine, at room temperature**
- **140 g / 5oz caster sugar**
- **170g / 6oz self-raising flour, sieved**
- **1 teaspoon vanilla essence**
- **some sultanas or chocolate chips to sprinkle on top (optional)**

Preheat oven to 400F / 200C / gas Mark 6.
Line small bun tins with 18 bun cases.
Mix eggs, margarine, sugar and sieved flour together until creamy. Mix in vanilla essence if liked.
Spoon batter into each bun case to about three-quarters full. If liked sprinkle some with sultanas or chocolate chips before baking. Bake for about 15 minutes until nicely risen and just cooked through.

120. Chocolate Faery Cakes

- 150g (5.5 oz) soft sunflower margarine
- 150 ml eggs (about 3)
- 150g (5.5 oz) caster sugar
- 55g (2 oz) cocoa powder
- 125g (4.5 oz) self-raising flour
- 70 ml milk, at room temperature
- 1 teaspoon vanilla essence
- 1 level teaspoon cream of tartar
- 1/2 level teaspoon bicarbonate of soda
- 1/2 level teaspoon glycerine

Preheat oven to 400F / 200C / gas Mark 6. Line bun tins with paper cases. Cream the margarine and sugar well. Mix in the sieved cocoa powder. Beat in eggs one at a time. Sieve together flour, bicarbonate of soda and cream of tartar and fold in lightly. Mix in milk and vanilla essence. Spoon into paper cases, about ¾ full. Bake for 12 to 15 minute until risen and springy to touch.

121. Little Honey Cakes

- 140g (5 oz) honey
- 140g (5 oz) sugar
- 2 tablespoons water
- 55g (2 oz) butter
- 1 egg
- 390 g (14 oz) plain flour
- 55g (2 oz) chopped flaked almonds
- zest of 1 orange
- zest of 1 lemon
- pinch of cinnamon, cloves, mixed spice, nutmeg and salt
- 1 rounded teaspoon bicarbonate of soda / bread soda

Optional glaze to add when still hot from the oven-
thin icing made with icing sugar and water

Gently melt together honey, sugar, water and butter and allow to cool slightly. Beat egg and add to the cooled mixture. Sieve flour and mix the remaining ingredients into a large bowl. Make a well in the centre and pour the melted honey mixture in, and stir until all mixed.

Using waxed paper roll into rough sausage shapes about 15cm / 6 inches long by 5cm / 2 inches wide. Put into fridge or freezer to chill. Cut into slices about 0.6 cm / ¼ inch thick and bake at 180C / 350F/ Gas Mark 4 about 10 minutes. While still very hot a mixture of icing sugar and water can be brushed on very thinly, though these are already very sweet.

122. Erin Cakes

- **225g (8 oz) plain flour**
- **1/2 teaspoon baking powder**
- **3 egg yolks**
- **1 egg white, stiffly beaten**
- **110g (4 oz) caster sugar**
- **55g (2 oz) butter at room temperature**
- **140 ml milk at room temperature**
- **pistachio nuts to decorate**
- **fondant icing sugar**
- **green food colouring**

Line a 20 cm / 8 inch square sandwich tin. Preheat the oven to 350F / 180C / Gas Mark 4.
Cream butter and sugar together until light and fluffy. Beat in the egg yolks one at a time along with the milk. Sieve the baking powder and flour into the mixture and fold in. Fold in the whipped egg white.
Transfer mixture to prepared tin and bake for 20 - 30 minutes until cooked through.
Turn out of tin and cool on a wire tray.
When fully cooled cut into diamond shapes. Make up some fondant icing according to pack instructions and colour it a pale green. Blanch a few pisctachio nuts, skin them, then cut into slices across the nut. Ice each diamond carefully, then put 3 pistachio nut slices together in the form of a shamrock on each cake. Add a strip of pistachio nut to form the stalk of the shamrock. Leave to set before serving.

Desserts & Puddings

123. Orange & Blackberry Pudding

- **335g (3/4 lb) blackberries**
- **28g (1 oz) butter**
- **110g (4 oz) caster sugar & some extra to sweeten blackberries**
- **2 large eggs, at room temperature, separated**
- **grated rind and all the juice of 1 small to medium sized orange**
- **55g (2 oz) self-raising flour**
- **powdered / icing sugar to dust**

Wash blackberries well. Line the bottom of an ovenproof dish with blackberries. Dust some sugar over these to sweeten (and form a sauce when cooked) and leave to soak in. In a separate bowl, cream butter with the sugar, add the egg yolks and beat well. Add orange rind and juice and mix through. Add flour and combine well. Beat egg whites until they form stiff peaks. Fold these well into the mixture. Pour all over the blackberries. Set the dish in a tray with about 2.5 cm / 1 inch of water surrounding it. Bake at 180 C / 350 F / Gas Mark 4 for 30 - 40 minutes until risen and golden.
Dust with powdered icing sugar to decorate.

124. Irish Honeycomb Cheesecake

Yellow Man is another word for hard honeycomb and is popular at fair days across Ireland. There are many recipes for yellow man, some of which are extremely hard on the teeth. This honeycomb recipe is much gentler, and is beautiful broken up into pieces and smothered in milk chocolate. It also tastes gorgeous in cheesecake. The quantity given here for honeycomb will make enough for one cheesecake, with some left over to cover in chocolate as a crunchy treat. Cover leftovers in chocolate the day you make your honeycomb as it will go quite gooey the next day if left exposed to the air. Make the honeycomb a couple of hours before you start to make the cheesecake. Or if you are short of time, just buy some ready-made honeycomb.

124b. Homemade Honeycomb Recipe

- **200g (7 oz) granulated / caster sugar**
- **45 ml (3 level tablespoons) honey**
- **30 ml (2 tablespoons) water**
- **1 level teaspoon bicarbonate of soda / bread soda**

Line a deep rectangular tray (one which will withstand hot temperatures) with greaseproof paper ready to pour boiling hot honeycomb into, or use a silicone mould. Put water, sugar and honey into a tall saucepan. Bring to a gentle boil, stirring until sugar and honey are dissolved. Continue to boil until mixture turns the colour of light golden honey, or until a little dropped into cold water forms a hard ball when rolled between the fingers. Be careful at this point not to over boil and burn the sugar, or boil too little which would cause the honeycomb to flop. As soon as hard ball stage is reached, remove from heat and whisk in the baking soda. Immediately pour into waiting container and leave to set and cool. Soak saucepan in water to prevent honeycomb leftovers setting hard.

Cheesecake Base

- **170g (6 oz) digestive biscuits**
- **85g (3 oz) butter or margarine**

Melt butter and combine with the biscuit crumbs.
Press into the base of a 20cm /8 inch removable base circular tin / pan.

Cheesecake Filling
- **40g (1.5 oz) icing sugar**
- **140g (5 oz) cream cheese**
- **300 ml double cream, whipped**
- **85g (3 oz) honeycomb, crushed + extra for decoration**
- **155g (5.5 oz) ready-made caramel**

Beat cream cheese to soften and smooth, then mix in the icing sugar and cream. Fold in crushed honeycomb and caramel. Chill cheesecake and decorate with crushed honeycomb just before serving.

125. Mint Choc Bubble Bar Cheesecake

- **250g (9 oz) crushed digestive biscuits**
- **125g (4.5 oz) butter**

- **200 g (7 oz) cream cheese (NOT light!)**
- **250mls (just under 1/2 pint) whipping cream**
- **125g (4.5 oz) icing sugar**
- **large bar of bubbly mint chocolate, crushed**

Melt margarine and mix well into crushed biscuits. Press into base of a loose bottomed flan tin and chill while making topping.
Beat cheese and icing sugar together.
Whip cream & fold into cheese & sugar mixture.
Add approximately half of the crushed mint chocolate bubble bar to the mixture, mix well.
Spread filling over base and sprinkle remainder of crushed chocolate on top. Chill. Eat!

126. Almond Rice Cream

- **280 ml (1/2 pint) milk**
- **85g (3 oz) ground rice**
- **approximately 3 x 15 ml level tablespoons caster sugar**
- **3 x 15 ml tablespoons high fruit juice content lemon or orange squash**
- **140 ml thick custard**
- **1 small teacupful stewed apples or rhubarb**
- **fresh raspberries or blackberries**
- **almond essence**
- **fruit to decorate**

Simmer the rice and milk until tender, then transfer to a bowl to cool. Whip in the custard and fruit squash to make a soft creamy consistency. If too thick add a little more fruit squash. Sweeten to taste with the sugar and add a few drops of almond essence. Mix the stewed fruit through the pudding and serve decorated with some fresh raspberries or blackberries.

127. Irish Bramley Apple Meringue Pudding

Apple Meringue was one of the first class sweets served to some of the wealthiest passengers in the world on Titanic's doomed maiden voyage in 1912.

Apple Meringue Base

- **3 large / 450g (1 lb) Bramley cooking apples, peeled and slice**
- **finely grated rind of half a lemon**
- **85g (3 oz) granulated sugar**
- **2 eggs, separated**
- **285 mls (1/2 pint) milk**
- **110g (4 oz) freshly made breadcrumbs**
- **1/2 teaspoon almond essence**

Set egg whites aside for making meringue later.
Warm the milk. Lightly beat the egg yolks and combine with the warm milk, apples, lemon rind, sugar, breadcrumbs and almond essence. Put into a 3.5 pint / 2 litre ovenproof dish and cover over with foil. Set a tray with some water in it on shelf below to create steam. Bake for 45 minutes to 1 hour at 180C /350 F / Gas Mark 4.

Meringue Topping

- **the 2 egg whites set aside earlier**
- **110g (4 oz) caster sugar**
- **small handful flaked almonds**
- **6 glacé cherries**

Beat the egg whites until they form stiff peaks.
Gently fold in the sugar. Spread over baked apple mixture.
Decorate with the flaked almonds and cherries.
Bake at 140C / 275F / Gas Mark 1, until set.

128. Irish Apple Sponge Pudding

An old favourite, Irish Apple Sponge Pudding may be made with Bramley cooking apples, or it's a great way to use up those spare apples in the fruit bowl. Just sweeten according to taste when you are stewing the apples.

Half fill an ovenproof dish (around 21cm / 8 inch in diameter) with stewed apples – peel and slice **670g (1.5 lb) apples, sweeten to taste**, add a table-spoon of water, and microwave on high till cooked to a soft consistency. You can also stew them in the traditional way in a saucepan on the hob.

To make sponge topping:
- **1 egg**
- **55g (2oz) soft margarine**
- **55g (2oz) soft brown sugar**
- **70g (2.5 oz) plain flour**
- **2 teaspoons baking powder**
- **pinch of salt**
- **1 tablespoon boiling water**

Cream the margarine and sugar together, add egg along with one spoonful of flour and mix well. Fold in remainder of flour with the pinch of salt, and water. Lastly, add baking powder. Pour over cooked apple and bake at 170 C / 325 F / Gas Mark 3 for 30 to 45 minutes, until golden brown.

129. Semolina Pudding

Comforting semolina pudding was baked ever so slow in Ireland on the range or in a pot by the fire.

- **560 ml (1 pint) milk**
- **28 g (1 oz) 2 x 15 ml level tablespoons caster sugar**
- **40 g (1.5 oz) 3 x slightly rounded tablespoons semolina**
- **1 teaspoon vanilla essence**
- **1 egg, separated**

Preheat the oven to 300F / 150C / gas Mark 2. Bring the milk to the boil and sprinkle on the semolina, then the vanilla essence. Simmer until the mixture thickens, add the sugar, and whisk in the egg yolk. Whisk the egg white stiffly and fold in to mixture. Pour into a buttered ovenproof pudding dish and bake slowly for an hour or more until light golden brown on top.

130. Baked Tapioca & Apple Pudding

- **55g (2 oz) seed pearl tapioca**
- **710 ml full cream milk**
- **40g (1.5 oz) 3 level tablespoons caster sugar**
- **a good pinch of salt**
- **225g (1/2 lb) 1 large Bramley apple (peeled weight)**
- **55 g (2 oz) granulated or caster sugar**
- **a knob of butter to grease bowl**

Grease a small ovenproof glass pudding dish well with butter. Soak the tapioca in the milk for 15 minutes. Bring to the boil, then reduce to a simmer for 15 minutes, stirring all the time. Turn off heat and add sugar and salt, mixing well. Leave to cool for 15 minutes.

When the tapioca has cooled down and thickened a little, fill the greased dish with sliced Bramley apples. Sprinkle with the sugar. Pour tapioca over the fruit. Bake for 30 - 45 minutes at 350F / 180C / Gas Mark 4.

Serve on its own or with a big dollop of whipped cream.

131. Bramley Apple Fool

- **450g (1 lb) Bramley cooking apples**
- **2 cloves**
- **brown sugar to sweeten**
- **whipped cream to serve**

Peel and core apples, cut into quarters, and put in a strong preserving jar with 2 cloves and enough water to cover the apples. Cover with lid and stand in a saucepan of water. Boil steadily until the apples are soft. Remove cloves and sieve or puree. Serve with whipped cream.

132. Steamed Rhubarb

Clean the **rhubarb** and cut it into 5 cm (2 inch) lengths. Set it in a stewing jar or basin along with a nice piece of **lemon rind**. Do not add any water to it. Cook in a steamer over boiling water until nearly tender. Add **sugar** to taste, return to the steamer and cook for a quarter of an hour.

133. Next Day Blackberries

The hedgerows in Irish fields and meadows are overladen with blackberries each autumn. You could pick all evening only to find you've completely run out of time and energy to bake the blackberries before nightfall. The next recipe preserves the fruit perfectly for baking or desserts, otherwise these wild fresh fruits could have formed a fur by the next morning and all your efforts would have been in vain. It freezes well and is an economical way of serving your favourite Greek yogurt with fruit compote on the side, costing a fraction of the price of single serving commercial varieties.

So on those occasions when you have run out of time, wash the blackberries, drain and put in a large saucepan with a little honey and sugar in the following proportions:

For each 450 g (1 lb) **blackberries** add 30 ml (2 tablespoons) **honey** and 55 g (2oz) **caster sugar.**

Cover the saucepan with a lid and cook gently for 5 to 10 minutes until soft. Allow to cool, then sieve the liquid from the blackberries and measure it out. Set the sieved blackberries to one side. For every 115 mls liquid dissolve 1.5 rounded teaspoons **ground arrowroot** in a little cold **water**. Bring the blackberry liquid back to a simmer, whisk in the dissolved ground arrowroot and simmer for just a few minutes until thickened. Leave the mixture to cool again. When cool add the drained blackberries.

Store in the fridge until the following day, or freeze in a rigid container for later use.

134. Bramble Duff Pudding

Filling:
- **450 g (1 lb) next day blackberry mixture (see previous recipe)**

Topping:
- **100 g (3.5 oz) self-raising flour**
- **3 teaspoons caster sugar**
- **1 teaspoon baking powder**
- **pinch of salt**
- **3 teaspoons soft baking margarine**
- **40 ml (8 teaspoons) milk at room temperature**

Put the blackberry mixture into a 1.25 or 1.5 litre microwaveable glass bowl. (If the blackberry mixture has been in the fridge bring to room temperature in the microwave.) Sieve the flour, baking powder, salt and sugar into a bowl and gently rub in the margarine with your fingertips. Add milk and bind together to form a soft dough.

Dust worktop with flour and pat the dough out gently to form a circle which will fit and cover the top of the blackberry mixture. Gently lay this on top, and cover with a vented microwave plate cover. Microwave on high for approximately 6 or 7 minutes until the duff topping is cooked and risen. Be careful to watch in the final minute or so of cooking, as if left for too long the fruit mixture will bubble up over the sides of the bowl.

135. Blackberry & Bramley Apple Autumn Pudding
(a version of Summer Pudding)

- **250 g (9 oz) Bramley cooking apples cut into medium sized diced chunks**
- **450 g (1 lb) blackberries**
- **125 g (4.5 oz) granulated sugar**
- **about 7 or 8 slices of a few days old white medium cut bread**

Line a 1.25 litre pudding bowl with clingfilm, allowing the cling film to come out well over the edge of the bowl.

Put the diced apple, blackberries, and sugar in a saucepan without adding water, and simmer gently for about 15 minutes. Set a sieve over a medium sized bowl and gently drain the juice from the fruit.

Remove crusts from bread and dip slices into the juice of the fruits for a few seconds, then line the base and the sides of the bowl with these, reserving enough for the top of the pudding.

Tip the fruit into the bread lined bowl and finish off the top of the pudding with the reserved slices of bread.

Cover over the pudding with cling film, set a side plate on top and set in the fridge with another weight on top. Leave to chill overnight.

Serve with whipped fresh cream or vanilla ice cream.

136. Wild Blackberry Dessert Jelly

This recipe would be a very expensive way just to make a pudding jelly if the blackberries had to be purchased in the supermarket. When wild blackberries are in abundance it's well worth the effort of making your own homemade fruit jelly.

- **450g (1 lb) wild blackberries**
- **85 g (3 oz) granulated sugar**
- **10 g (0.35 oz) leaf gelatine**

Leave the gelatine to soak in cold water. Wash the blackberries, shaking off any excess water, and put in a saucepan with the sugar.
Heat slowly until the blackberry juices begin to run, then simmer for about 10 minutes. Push through a sieve to extract the juice, crushing the berries with a spoon.
Measure the juice and make up to 560 ml (1 pint) with water.
Put this back in the saucepan, drain the gelatine and add to the juice.
Gently melt for a few minutes, whisk, and transfer to jelly mould or bowl to set.

137. Early 20th century old Blackberry Roll recipe

- **110 g (4 oz) plain flour**
- **2 teaspoons baking powder**
- **¼ teaspoon salt**
- **80 ml milk**
- **2 x 15 ml rounded tablespoons shortening**

Filling
- **200 g (7 oz) blackberries sweetened with 85 g (3 oz) sugar**

Optional Topping –
- **A little vanilla flavoured glace icing to drizzle over the baked roll**

Preheat oven to 350°F / 180°C / Gas Mark 4.
Sieve the flour, baking powder and salt together. Rub the shortening in finely to resemble fine breadcrumbs. Add as much of the milk as is needed to form a soft dough. Roll out to 6 mm /1/4 inch thickness. Spread with the sweetened blackberries and roll up.

138. Stewed Blackberries and Apple

- **110 g (4 oz) blackberries, washed**
- **225 g (1/2 lb) 1 large Bramley cooking apple**
- **1 or 2 teaspoons granulated sugar (or sweeten according to taste)**
- **30 ml / 2 tablespoons water**

Put the blackberries and water in a saucepan.
Peel the cooking apple and cut into slivers using a vegetable peeler or knife.
Add to the saucepan and bring to a slow simmer.
Cover the saucepan and cook until tender.
Add a little sugar to taste.
Serve with custard, ice cream or Greek yogurt.

139. Hot Apple & Blackberry Trifle

Base layer
- **85g (3 oz) trifle sponges / sponge cake**
- **170g (6 oz) frozen blackberries**
- **5 tablespoons water**
- **3 tablespoons sugar**

Second Layer
- **2 large Bramley cooking apples - 450g (1 lb) net weight after peeling**
- **85g (3 oz) sugar**
- **3 tablespoons water**

Third layer
- **560 ml (1 pint) vanilla custard**

Meringue Topping
- **2 egg whites**
- **55g (2 oz) caster sugar**

Crumble the sponge into an ovenproof dish. Cook the blackberries gently in the water and sugar for three minutes. Spoon over the sponge base. Cook the apples with the sugar and water until soft. Put in a layer on top of the blackberry mixture. Put a layer of custard on top. Whisk the egg whites until stiff. Gradually whisk in the caster sugar. Spoon or pipe over the custard and bake at 325F / 170C / Gas Mark 3 until golden.

140. Wild Blackberry Topping (for yogurt or cheesecake)

- **500g (1 lb 2oz) freshly picked wild blackberries**
- **finely grated rind and juice of half a medium-sized sweet orange**
- **2 tablespoons soft light brown sugar**
- **6 tablespoons good quality red wine**
- **a few teaspoons cornflour (cornstarch) to thicken to your liking**

Put the first 4 ingredients in a saucepan and simmer gently for about 20 minutes. Pass the mixture through a sieve extracting as much juice as possible. Mix the cornflour in a little cold water. Return the fruit juice to the saucepan and, over a gentle heat, add cornflour mixture to thicken the fruit juice according to taste.

141. Irish Bread & Butter Pudding
Serves 2

- **4 slices of Irish fruit loaf, buttered, crusts removed**
- **1 large egg**
- **235 ml milk**
- **2 tablespoons light brown sugar**
- **freshly grated nutmeg**

Cut buttered fruit loaf slices into small squares, and place in a small, buttered ovenproof pudding bowl or dish. Whisk eggs and milk together well, pour over the bread. Press down a little and leave to sit for about 5 minutes. Sprinkle with a little grated nutmeg and the light brown sugar. Bake for 30 – 45 minutes at 180C / 350F / Gas Mark 4.

Tip - Serving Summer Fruits

When serving a simple platter of summer fruits such as Irish strawberries or raspberries, put a shallow glass dish filled with broken ice in the centre of the serving platter and dress the fruit neatly around it. This keeps the fruit cool without coming into contact with the ice. A few green leaves or one or two edible flowers help set the dish off.

142. Almond Topped Gooseberry Pie

- **335g (3/4 lb) frozen gooseberries, defrosted**
- **55g (2 oz) soft butter / margarine**
- **110g (4 oz) caster sugar + extra to sprinkle on gooseberries**
- **2 eggs, separated**
- **55g (2 oz) ground almonds**
- **55g (2 oz) self-raising flour**
- **a few drops of almond essence**
- **280 ml (1/2 pint) milk**

Heat oven to 190C / 375F / Gas Mark 5. Put gooseberries in a greased, oven-proof dish. Sprinkle a handful of sugar over berries. Beat butter and sugar, then beat in egg yolks. Fold in flour and ground almonds. Stir in almond essence and milk. Whisk egg whites until they form stiff peaks. Fold these into the mixture. Spoon mixture over gooseberries.
Place dish in a roasting tin half filled with water.
Bake for 40 – 45 minutes until golden brown and spongy to touch.
(Lower the temperature if the top is browning too fast before the mixture has set).
Serve hot with whipped cream.

143. Sticky Toffee Sauce
This sauce is lovely poured over toffee or golden syrup cake and baked for 20 minutes in the oven - a simple, easy, sticky toffee pudding.

- **55g (2 oz) butter**
- **110g (4 oz) soft brown sugar**
- **110g (4 oz) golden syrup**
- **1 teaspoon vanilla extract**
- **140 ml (1/4 pint) fresh cream**

Put all ingredients into a saucepan and bring to the boil.
Boil for 5 minutes if rebaking in a toffee pudding, a little longer to make a toffee sauce for ice cream.

144. Border of Rice with Plums

- **110g (4 oz) ground rice**
- **1135 ml milk**
- **55g (2 oz) butter**
- **55g (2 oz) caster sugar**
- **2 egg yolks**
- **1 bay leaf or vanilla essence**
- **ready prepared plum or other fruit compote (see next recipe)**

Grease a border pudding mould well with butter and set aside. If you don't have a border mould use a regular one and set an oiled jam jar half filled with water in the centre to create a hollow.

Moisten the ground rice with some of the cold milk, boil the remainder with the bayleaf or vanilla essence, then pour it over the rice. Return all to the saucepan. Add the butter and boil all until thick. As the mixture is thickening add the sugar and egg yolks, stirring well. Remove the bayleaf. Pour into the buttered pudding mould; when cold, turn out on a glass dish and fill the centre with a compote of plums.

145. Fruit Compote

In a true fruit compote the syrup must be rich, thick, and well flavoured, the fruit in slices or whole, but in both cases unbroken.

The amount of sugar used is dependent on the acidity of the fruit:-

For acidic fruit
- **280g (10 oz) sugar**
- **280 ml (1/2 pint) of water OR half claret or sherry and half water**
- **a piece of lemon peel OR a cinnamon stick**

Boil sugar in water OR half claret or sherry and half water, for 10 minutes. A piece of lemon peel or a cinnamon stick gives flavour depending on the fruit used. Add the fruit and simmer very gently until sufficiently cooked. Carefully lift out the fruit and put it in a dish. Quickly boil the syrup to reduce it in quantity, then pour it over the fruit. A little natural red colouring may also be added.

For sweet fruits use 170g (6 oz) of sugar per pound.

146. Rhubarb Crumble

- **500g (1 lb 2 oz) sticks of rhubarb**
- **170g (6 oz) granulated or caster sugar**

Crumble
- **170g (6 oz) plain flour**
- **85g (3 oz) butter**
- **55g (2 oz) granulated or caster sugar**

Preheat oven to 375 F / 190 C / Gas Mark 5. Cut rhubarb sticks into small pieces and put in base of ovenproof dish. Sprinkle with sugar.

Make crumble topping -
Rub butter into flour until it looks like fine breadcrumbs. Add sugar and sprinkle crumble over fruit in bowl.
Put in oven and cook for 15 minutes. Turn heat down to 325 F / 170 C / Gas Mark 3 and bake for another 45 minutes or so until golden and rhubarb is well cooked. Serve with custard or whipped cream.

147. Bramloffee Pie
An Irish Bramley apple toffee version of the classic Banoffee Pie

Base
- **110g (4 oz) butter or margarine**
- **250g (9 oz) crushed digestive biscuits**

Caramel Filling
- **110g (4 oz) butter**
- **110g (4 oz) soft brown sugar**
- **395g (14 oz) sweetened condensed milk**
- **2 large Bramley apples, stewed and sweetened to taste, chilled**
- **140 ml (1/4 pint) double or whipping cream**

 Mix the melted butter with the biscuit crumbs. Press into a loose bottomed pie plate or flan dish, and leave to set (can chill it in fridge to speed up setting).

Melt the butter and brown sugar together, stirring well until all dissolved. Add the sweetened condensed milk and boil until you have a golden caramel, stirring all the time. Allow to cool slightly then pour evenly over pie base. Leave to set, transferring to fridge to chill as soon as toffee has cooled. Cover toffee evenly with the stewed Bramley apples. Decorate with chilled whipped cream just before serving.

148. Potato Apple

For potato apple to work you must use Bramley cooking apples. Their unique flavour is essential for this Orchard County favourite.

- **225g (8 oz) 2 medium sized potatoes boiled, mashed and riced**
- **28g (1 oz) butter**
- **85g (3 oz) plain flour**

Filling:
- **140g (5 oz) 1 large Bramley cooking apple**
- **sugar to taste**
- **a knob of butter**

Make a quantity of plain potato bread in the normal way i.e. boil potatoes and mash them while still hot. Put through a potato ricer. Add the butter and salt and then mix in the flour to form a soft dough. Weigh into 2 even sized pieces. On a floured worktop, roll each piece out into a circle of about 15 cm / 6 inches in diameter. Peel and core the apples and chop them into small dice. Spread the apple evenly over one circle leaving a little space around the outside. Set the second circle on top and seal around the edges with your thumbs. Slide potato apple onto a lightly heated griddle. (There is no need to grease the griddle as the butter which was mashed into the potatoes is sufficient). Gently cook for about 5 minutes or until lightly browned. Carefully turn over to the other side. Cut a 9cm / 3.5 inch circle out of the top of the potato apple. Sprinkle in enough sugar to sweeten. Add a knob of butter and replace lid. Continue to cook for another 5 minutes or so, until the base is lightly browned. Serve hot, sprinkled with a little more sugar if desired.

149. Potato Pudding

- **450g (1 lb) about 6 medium, warm, boiled potatoes, mashed and riced**
- **110g (4oz) butter**
- **85g (3oz) light brown sugar**
- **55g (2 oz) caster sugar**
- **55g (2 oz) self-raising flour**
- **2 beaten eggs**
- **pinch of salt**
- **1 rounded teaspoon of mixed spice**
- **2 medium eating apples**
- **a little warm milk to mix**
- **greaseproof paper, tin foil and string to cover pudding dish**

Grease a 2 litre ovenproof glass bowl well.

Prepare the potatoes and beat in butter. Peel, core and dice the apples.

Combine all ingredients together in a bowl, adding a little warmed milk if necessary, to make a thick batter.

Transfer pudding batter to ovenproof bowl. Cover bowl with a circle of greaseproof paper and tinfoil on top, tied well with string. Put a tray of warm water in oven. Place bowl on top and steam at 325F / 170C / Gas Mark 3 for 2 hours.

150. Cheat's Irish Christmas Plum Pudding in a Flash

If all else fails and you find yourself with no plum pudding on Christmas day, you can knock this one up in a flash. Give it your own signature by adding some extra favourite nuts or dried fruit.

Stir 235 ml of **Irish stout**, a few drops of **cake browning** and one **beaten egg** into a 430g (15.5 oz) jar of **good quality mincemeat**. Add another small handful of **chopped walnuts / pecan nuts** or anything else you would like in your plum pudding. Add 110g (4 oz) **flour** and 110g (4 oz) **breadcrumbs.** Mix well together. Put in a microwaveable glass bowl, cover with a vented microwave cover and microwave on high for 8 to 10 minutes or until just nicely cooked through.

Serve smothered in **hot custard** and **ice cold whipped cream.**

151. Christmas Pudding

- 110g (4 oz) fine breadcrumbs (brown or white)
- 225ml hot water
- 310g (11 oz) brown sugar
- 40g (1.5 oz) ground almonds
- 335g (12 oz) butter, melted
- 6 eggs
- 85g (3 oz) 3 tablespoons treacle
- 1 teaspoon lemon essence
- 225g (8 oz) plain flour
- 1 teaspoon ground mixed spice
- 1/2 teaspoon freshly grated nutmeg
- 950g (2 lb. 2 oz) sultanas
- 335g (12oz) currants
- 55g (2oz) finely chopped candied peel
- 55g (2 oz) stem ginger in sugar syrup, drained and finely chopped
- 85g (3 oz) glacé cherries
- 85g (3 oz) flaked almonds
- 85g (3 oz) walnuts, roughly chopped

Put sultanas and currants into a bowl and cover with warm water. Leave to steep half an hour, then drain well, discarding the water. In another bowl mix the breadcrumbs with the measured out amount of hot water. Add the brown sugar, ground almonds, and melted butter and mix all together well. Beat the eggs and add these to the breadcrumb mixture along with the treacle and lemon essence and mix all together until combined.
Weigh out the flour and blend in the mixed spice and nutmeg. Add these to the breadcrumb and egg mixture. Next add the fruits, ginger and nuts and mix together well. Put into 3 well-greased 2 pint / 1.125 litre pudding basins, cover and set in the oven in a deep pan filled with water. Bake between 150 – 170C / 300 -325F / Gas Mark 2 -3 for about 1 hr. 45 minutes.

152. Brandy Butter

- 225g (8 oz) butter
- 110g (4 oz) icing sugar
- 1 or 2 tablespoons brandy, according to taste

Cream the butter well, add the icing sugar and brandy to taste. Chill until firm and serve cut into shapes on a little serving dish.

153. Christmas Crumble

- **420g (15 oz) about 6 or 7 medium apples, peeled, cored and diced**
- **420g (15 oz) jar sweet mincemeat**

Topping:
- **225g (8 oz) cups plain flour**
- **85g (3 oz) light brown sugar**
- **55g (2 oz) butter**
- **1 level teaspoon ground cloves**

Mix apples and sweet mincemeat well together and put into an ovenproof dish approximate size 22.5 cm / 9 inch diameter and 7.5 cm /3 inches deep.

To make the topping:
Chop butter into small pieces and rub into the flour until it resembles fine breadcrumbs. Mix in the light brown sugar and ground cloves. Sprinkle across top of the fruit and bake slowly at 180C / 350F / Gas Mark 4 for 45 minutes – 1 hour. Serve warm.

154. Buttermilk Dumpling

- **225g (1/2 lb) plain flour**
- **110g (4 oz) suet**
- **55g (2 oz) sultanas**
- **55g (2 oz) large raisins**
- **55g (2 oz) lemon peel**
- **28g (1 oz) citron**
- **1 rounded teaspoon sweet spice**
- **1 level teaspoon cinnamon**
- **85g (3 oz) sugar**
- **1 rounded teaspoon bicarbonate of soda /bread soda**
- **buttermilk to mix**

Combine all dry ingredients and add as much buttermilk as will make dough stiff, but soft.
Transfer to a pudding basin and steam for 4 hours.

155. Jam Sauce for Plain Sponge Puddings

- **2 heaped tablespoonfuls raspberry jam**
- **28g (1 oz) sugar**
- **140 ml (1/4 pint) water**
- **lemon juice**

Put sugar and water on to boil; boil 10 minutes; add jam, lemon juice; boil up, and sieve round pudding.

156. Hot Whiskey Sauce for Puddings

- **110g (4 oz) demerara sugar**
- **110g (4 oz) butter**
- **75ml double cream**
- **3 tablespoons Irish whiskey**
- **3 tablespoons lemon juice**
- **pinch of ground cloves**

Put butter, sugar and cloves in a saucepan and simmer until the butter melts and the sugar dissolves. Stir in the cream and bring to the boil. Reduce the heat and simmer for 5-7 minutes, stirring continuously and allowing the sauce to reduce and thicken.

Remove from the heat and beat in the whiskey and lemon juice. This sauce thickens as it cools.

157. Semolina Jelly

- 1 packet of fruit jelly crystals or tablet of jelly which makes 1 pint
- 28 g (1 oz) ground semolina
- 560 ml (1 pint) boiling water

Melt the jelly in the boiling water and whisk in the semolina. Simmer in a saucepan or cook in the microwave for 7 minutes, whisking well through-out cooking time. Transfer to a bowl or mould and leave to cool completely, whisking every so often as it cools. Chill and leave to set. Serve with freshly whipped cream and lots of fruit.

158. Sago Pudding with Bramble Jelly

- 1.5 tablespoons sago
- 560 ml (1 imperial pint) milk
- 1 egg, separated
- 1 teaspoon caster sugar + extra for dusting
- bramble jelly
- freshly grated nutmeg

Preheat oven to 375F / 190C / Gas Mark 5. Wash sago well and simmer in milk for about 10 minutes until thickened. Cool. Beat the egg yolk with one teaspoon of caster sugar and one tablespoon of the milk. Stir gently into the sago. Beat the egg white stiffly and fold in. Bake in a greased ovenproof dish for 15 minutes or until top is lightly browned. Dust a little caster sugar and grated nutmeg over top of pudding, and serve with the bramble jelly.

159. Redcurrant Bread & Butter Pudding

- 335g (12 oz) redcurrants
- 12 slices of stale bread
- 55g (2 oz) butter
- 560 ml (1 Imperial pint) milk
- 1 teaspoon vanilla essence
- 2 eggs
- 6 tablespoons caster sugar

Wash and drain the redcurrants. Remove the stalks. Remove the crusts from the bread. Spread with butter and cut into triangles.

Sprinkle a few redcurrants over the bottom of a well-greased ovenproof dish and arrange some of the bread on top. Cover with redcurrants, then a layer of bread. Repeat the layers.

Put the milk and vanilla essence into a saucepan and bring to the boil. Remove from the heat. Whisk the eggs with 5 tablespoons of the sugar till frothy, then pour in the hot milk, whisking continuously. Strain the custard over the redcurrants and bread. Leave to soak for 20 minutes.

Preheat the oven to 350F / 180C / Gas Mark 4.

Sprinkle the remaining sugar over the pudding and bake for about 40 minute until golden. Serve immediately with custard or whipped cream.

160. Irish Coffee Dessert Cake

The ultimate in retro decadence. You can freeze this in individual portions ready for unexpected visitors, or just for times when a little indulgence is called for.

- **125 g (4.5 oz) butter or margarine, at room temperature**
- **200g (7 oz) caster sugar**
- **2 large or 3 small eggs, separated**
- **90 ml (6 tablespoons) milk**
- **125g (4.5 oz) plain flour**
- **55g (2 oz) cornflour**
- **3 teaspoons baking powder**

Irish Coffee Syrup
- **140 ml strong black coffee**
- **110 g (4 oz) demerara sugar**
- **45 ml (3 tablespoons) Irish whiskey**

To decorate
- **250 ml double cream**
- **1 tablespoon vanilla pudding powder (optional - stabilises the cream)**
- **110g (4 oz) flaked almonds, toasted**

Grease and line a 20 cm / 8 inch cake tin. Preheat oven to 375F / 170C / Gas Mark 5.

Cream butter and sugar together until light and fluffy. Fold in sieved cornflour.

Gradually beat in the egg yolks and milk.

Add sieved flour and baking powder. Stiffly beat egg whites and fold in. Spoon into prepared tin.

Bake for 20 minutes, then lower oven temperature to 325F / 170C /Gas Mark 3 and bake for a further 20 - 30 minutes until cooked through. Turn out of tin and cool on a wire tray.

When cool return the cake (upside down) to the tin it was cooked in and prick all over with a fine skewer. (if you don't have one don't worry, it isn't essential to do this).

Make the coffee syrup - put the coffee and sugar in a saucepan. Stir until the sugar has dissolved, then boil for 5 minutes. Remove from the heat and stir in the whiskey. Pour the hot syrup over the cake ad leave to soak in. When cold, cover and leave overnight.

Next day whip the cream - if you are freezing the cake and wish to stabilise the cream whip in a tablespoon of vanilla pudding powder (found in sachets in the World Foods aisle of most supermarkets) at the stage where cream is just beginning to thicken.

Decorate with whipped cream and toasted flaked almonds.

161. Irish Coffee Jelly

- 420 ml (3/4 imperial pint) best quality strong black coffee
- 2 tablespoons caster sugar
- 1 x 12g (1/2 oz) sachet powdered gelatine
- 140 ml (1/4 imperial pint) Irish whiskey
- 280 ml (1/2 imperial pint) double cream

Put the coffee into a saucepan with the sugar and powdered gelatine. Simmer until dissolved. Remove from the heat and stir in the whiskey. Transfer to one large serving dish, or individual dessert dishes. When cool put in fridge and leave to set. When set decorate with piped whipped cream.

Traybakes - Irish favourites

162. Pineapple Delights

Base layer
- **225g (8 oz) crushed digestive biscuits**
- **110g (4 oz) butter or margarine**

Melt butter or margarine a little and add to crushed biscuits. Press into a swiss roll tin and chill.

Topping 1
- **28 g (1oz) soft margarine**
- **1 teaspoon water**
- **1/2 teaspoon vanilla essence**
- **140g (5 oz) sieved icing sugar**

Slightly melt margarine with water and vanilla essence.
Mix in the sieved icing sugar until creamy.
Spread this evenly across the chilled biscuit base.

Toppings 2 & 3
- **200 g (7 oz) drained, crushed pineapple**
- **240 ml fresh whipping cream**
- **grated chocolate or crushed ginger nut biscuits to decorate, if liked**

Spread half the pineapple evenly across creamed base.

Whip the cream and mix the rest of the pineapple into it.
Spread evenly across the top of the traybake. Decorate with grated chocolate or crushed ginger nut biscuits if desired. Chill and cut into squares to serve.

163. Mum's Fruit Squares

Pastry
- **225g (8oz) plain flour**
- **170g (6 oz) butter**
- **pinch of salt**
- **1 egg**
- **water to mix**
- **a little extra sugar to sprinkle on top**

Filling
- **225g (8 oz) currants, raisins and sultanas mixed**
- **110g (4 oz) sugar**
- **1 apple**
- **1 level teaspoon cinnamon**
- **1 level teaspoon mixed spice**
- **280mls (1/2 pint) water**
- **1 dessertspoon cornflour / cornstarch**

Grease a 30 x 20 cm / 12 x 8 inch swiss roll tin.

To make pastry:

Rub margarine into flour until it resembles fine breadcrumbs. Beat egg slightly. Mix egg and a little water into flour mixture to form a stiff dough. Leave in fridge to chill.

To make filling:

Put fruits, sugar, water and chopped peeled apple in a saucepan. Bring to boil and add mixed spice and cinnamon. Dissolve cornflour in a little cold water and add to saucepan. Boil again until mixture thickens. Allow to cool down. Preheat oven to 200C /400F /Gas Mark 6.

Divide pastry in half. Roll out half to cover base of Swiss roll tin. Spread fruit filling on top. Cover with other half of the pastry and sprinkle a little sugar across the top. Bake until golden brown. Cut into squares when cold.

164. Oaten Apple Slice

- 110g (4 oz) porridge oats
- 140g (5 oz) plain flour
- a good pinch of bicarbonate of soda / bread soda
- a good pinch of salt
- 110g (4 oz) light brown sugar
- 110 g (4 oz) melted butter
- 365 g (13 oz) sliced eating apples
- 1/4 level teaspoon ground cinnamon
- 2 tablespoons caster sugar

Preheat oven to 180C / 350F / Gas Mark 4. Put oats, flour, bicarbonate of soda, salt, light brown sugar, and melted butter in a large bowl and mix well. Press half of this mixture evenly across the bottom of a 21cm / 8 inch loose bottomed circular cake tin. Toss the sliced apples, ground cinnamon, and caster sugar together in a bowl. Lay these evenly across the base. Sprinkle the rest of the oat mixture evenly over the top, flattening it down a little. Bake for approximately 45 minutes until a nice golden colour.

165. Paradise Squares

- 110g (4 oz) ready-made shortcrust pastry
- seedless raspberry jam
- 110g (4oz) caster sugar
- 110g (4 oz) margarine
- 85g (3 oz) ground almonds
- 2 eggs
- 85g (3 oz) glace cherries, quartered
- 55g (2 oz) self-raising flour
- 55g (2 oz) ground rice

Preheat oven to 190C / 375F / Gas Mark 5. Line a swiss roll tin with pastry. Cover with a skimming of the jam. Cream margarine and sugar, add beaten eggs with one spoonful of the flour, and mix together. Mix rest of dry ingredients with cherries and add to mixture. Spread over jam base. Bake in oven until just springy to touch. Sprinkle with caster sugar and cut into squares.

166. *Marshmallow Crispy Squares*

- **125g (4.5 oz) 16 marshmallows**
- **110g (4 oz) puffed rice breakfast cereal**
- **200g (7 oz) slab toffee or budget buy toffee sweets**
- **55g (2 oz) margarine**

Melt toffee, marshmallows and margarine gently. Remove from heat, check that mixture is not so hot that it would soften the puffed rice, then mix all together well. Press into lightly greased tin. Cut into squares.

167. *Fifteens*
No oven needed. The first 4 ingredient quantities tell how they got their title.

- **240g (8.5 oz) 15 crushed digestive biscuits**
- **15 glace cherries, halved**
- **15 pink and white marshmallows**
- **15 walnut pieces**
- **225g (8 oz) sweetened condensed milk**
- **85g (3 oz) desiccated coconut**

Put digestive biscuits in a plastic bag and crush with a rolling pin. In a bowl mix crushed biscuits, halved cherries, chopped walnut pieces, marshmallows torn into small pieces, and sweetened condensed milk.
Dust worktop with desiccated coconut and roll mixture in it to form a log shape. Wrap this in cling film and chill for 2 hours in fridge or overnight at room temperature. Slice into 15 pieces and serve.

168. *Almond Slices*
(fills one Swiss roll tin, 8 x 12 inch / 20 cm x 30 cm)

Pastry:
Use ready rolled, or make your own –
- **170g (6 oz) plain flour**
- **85g (3 oz) margarine**
- **40g (1.5 oz) caster sugar**
- **1 small egg beaten**
- **seedless jam to spread over base (raspberry or apricot are good)**

Preheat oven to 200C / 400F / Gas Mark 6. Rub margarine finely into flour. Mix 2/3 of the beaten egg with caster sugar to make a paste. Combine this with the flour mixture, adding the last of the whipped egg if necessary, to make a soft dough. Roll out on a well-floured worktop and line base of Swiss roll tin, saving any leftover pastry to make a few little pies or jam tarts with. Spread base lightly with some seedless jam.

Make Almond Filling
- **110g (4 oz) caster sugar**
- **110g (4oz) icing sugar, sieved**
- **110g (4 oz) ground almonds**
- **55g (2 oz) semolina**
- **1 whole egg + 1 egg white, whisked with 1 level teaspoon almond essence**
- **a handful of flaked almonds to sprinkle over top**

Mix together first 4 dry ingredients, then bind with whisked egg mixture. Lay evenly over jam base and sprinkle flaked almonds over the top. Bake for 20 – 30 minutes.
Allow to cool a little and cut into squares or slices.

169. Marie's Bars

- **110g (4 oz) margarine**
- **200g (7 oz) sweetened condensed milk**
- **110 g (4 oz) desiccated coconut**
- **225g (8 oz) marie biscuits, broken into small pieces**
- **7 cherries, chopped into smal pieces**
- **85g (3 oz) mini marshmallows**
- **170g (6 oz) white chocolate**

Melt margarine and condensed milk. Add coconut and cook for 1 minute. Remove from heat, add broken biscuits and mini marshmallows. Press into a swiss roll tin and leave to firm. Cover with melted white chocolate and cut into squares or bars when set.

170. Ginger Sponge Squares

- **235 ml milk**
- **4 x 15 ml level tablespoons golden syrup**
- **110g (4 oz) butter**
- **225g (8 oz) self-raising flour**
- **225g (8 oz) sugar**
- **2 heaped teaspoons ground ginger**
- **1 rounded teaspoon bicarbonate of soda**
- **1 egg, whisked**

Line a 25cm / 9 inch square tin (depth 5cm / 2 inches) with greaseproof paper. Preheat oven to 170C / 325F / Gas Mark 3. Melt milk, golden syrup and butter together in a saucepan and let cool. Weigh out the self raising flour, sugar, ground ginger, and bicarbonate of soda and sieve them into a bowl. Combine dry ingredients with melted mixture. Add whisked egg and mix all together. Transfer to prepared tin and bake for about 45 minutes until cooked through. Cut into squares to serve.

171. Bride's Slices

- **ready rolled or 1 x pastry recipe such as almond slices pastry**
- **seedless raspberry jam to cover base with a thin layer**
- **55g (2 oz) margarine**
- **110g (4 oz) caster sugar**
- **2 beaten eggs**
- **170g (6 oz) crushed digestive biscuits**
- **225g (8 oz) dried fruit**
- **110g (4 oz) glace cherries**
- **1 teaspoon mixed spice**
- **a little apricot jam**
- **250g (9 oz) ready-made almond icing**
- **250g (9 oz) ready-made royal icing**

Line Swiss roll tin with pastry , and cover with a thin layer of raspberry jam. Cream the margarine and sugar together, mix in the beaten eggs, then add the fruit, crushed digestive biscuits, cherries and mixed spice. Bake at 350°F for 30 to 35 minutes. Leave to cool. When cool, spread a fine layer of apricot jam on top. Next add a layer of almond paste, finishing off with a layer of white royal icing on top. Cut into squares or slices.

172. Mallow Snowballs

- **170 g (6 oz) digestive biscuits**
- **150g (5 .5 oz) packet of pink & white Marshmallows**
- **2 tablespoons drinking chocolate**
- **55g (2 oz) margarine**
- **195g (7 oz) sweetened condensed milk**
- **dessicated coconut – enough to roll mallow snowballs in**

Crush biscuits finely, add drinking chocolate and melted margarine. Stir in condensed milk. Dampen hands in cold water and shape 1 heaped teaspoon of mix into a round pancake shape. Place mallow in centre and work the mixture around it to form a ball. Roll in coconut and leave to set in a cool place.

173. Lemon Coconut Slices

Base
- **110g (4 oz) margarine**
- **225g (8 oz) crushed Marie or Rich Tea biscuits**
- **85g (3 oz) desiccated coconut**
- **195g (7 oz) sweetened condensed milk**
- **finely grated rind of a lemon**
Topping
- **55g (2 oz) butter**
- **225g (8 oz) icing sugar**
- **juice of half the lemon**
- **lemon colouring, if desired**
- **desiccated coconut to sprinkle on top**

Melt margarine and condensed milk. Stir in the crushed biscuits, desiccated coconut and lemon rind. Press into a 30 x 20cm / 12 x 8 inch swiss roll tin. Cream topping ingredients together until light and fluffy. Spread evenly over the base and mark a pattern with a fork if liked. Sprinkle a little coconut over the top and cut into squares or slices. If preferred, lemon or white glace icing-may be used instead of buttercream.

174. Biscuit Fudge

- **110g (4 oz) margarine**
- **200g (7 oz) sweetened condensed milk**
- **110g (4 oz) sugar**
- **335g (12 oz) crushed digestive biscuits**
- **2 tablespoons syrup**
- **chocolate to cover**

Melt margarine, sugar, syrup and condensed milk and bring to the boil. Cook until the mixture turns golden Cool slightly and add crushed biscuits. Spread into a swiss roll tin. Leave to set, then cover with melted chocolate. When cool cut into squares or small bars.

175. Chocolate Peppermint Squares

Base:
- **110g (4 oz) margarine**
- **55g (2 oz) caster sugar**
- **55g (2 oz) plain flour**
- **1/2 teaspoon baking powder**
- **110g (4 oz) desiccated coconut**
- **2 level tablespoons drinking chocolate**

Filling:
- **55g (2 oz) margarine**
- **110g (4 oz) icing sugar**
- **peppermint essence**
- **green colouring**

Topping:
- **chocolate to cover**

Make base by creaming the margarine and sugar until light. Add dry base ingredients and bake for 20 - 30 minutes at 180C / 350F / Gas Mark 4. Leave aside to cool.
Make peppermint filling - beat together margarine and icing sugar; add a few drops of peppermint essence and green colour to give a mint green shade. Cover with melted chocolate and allow to set. Cut into squares.

176. Oaten Shortbread

- 110g (4 oz) margarine
- 55g (2 oz) soft brown sugar
- 110g (4 oz) flaked oats
- 85g (3 oz) plain flour
- 1/4 teaspoon bicarbonate of soda
- a pinch of salt

Grease a 17.5 cm (7 inch) square baking tin. Preheat oven to 350F / 180C / Gas Mark 4. Melt margarine and mix in remaining ingredients. Spread evenly in greased tin and press down firmly with the back of a dessert spoon. Bake for 30 - 45 minutes. Cut into fingers or squares while hot.

177. Celtic Tiger Shortbread

Base
- 170g (6 oz) self-raising flour
- 55 g (2oz) caster sugar
- 110g (4 oz) butter

Filling
- 110g (4 oz) butter
- 110g (4 oz) soft brown sugar
- 2 level tablespoons golden syrup
- 200g (7 oz) sweetened condensed milk
- 1/2 teaspoon vanilla essence

Topping
- 110g (4 oz) white or milk chocolate

Sieve flour and sugar into a bowl and rub in the butter until the mixture resembles fine breadcrumbs. Bind together and press evenly into a 20 cm (8 inch) square tin.

Bake at 180C / 350F / Gas Mark 4 for 25 - 30 minutes until golden.

Put all filling ingredients in a saucepan or microwaveable bowl. Dissolve and then boil gently, or microwave in bursts of 1 minute, stirring regularly, for about 7 minutes until caramel is formed. Spread caramel over cooked base and leave aside to cool.

When cool melt chocolate gently and spread evenly over top of filling. When set cut into squares.

178. Chapel Windows

- **225g (8 oz) broken biscuits**
- **110g (4 oz) margarine**
- **110g (4 oz) sugar**
- **55g (2 oz) drinking chocolate**
- **1 beaten egg**
- **28g (1 oz) raisins**
- **110g (4 oz) white or milk chocolate**

Melt margarine and sugar in a saucepan, add drinking chocolate and mix well. Whisk in beaten egg and simmer for 30 seconds. Remove from heat and mix in broken biscuits and raisins.

Press into a swiss roll tin and cover with melted chocolate. Leave to set and mark into squares.

179. Granny's Favourite Traybake

Perched in the back of our blue Vauxhall Viva in my handknit emerald Aran cardi and periwinkle blue pinafore dress, I would dream of the traybakes which were guaranteed when we arrived at Granny's. Lined up in neat rows I could see them waiting, and taste the pale icing as I bit down through the broken rich tea biscuits, bound with their sticky mix of chocolate malt, brown sugar, cherries and coconut. As a child I didn't realise they were made from the barley malt and cocoa powder that Granny loved to put in her hot milk; the secret to the unique taste of these unusual traybakes.

- **225g (8oz) Rich Tea biscuits, broken**
- **110 g (4 oz) firm baking margarine**
- **110g (4 oz) soft brown sugar**
- **2 level tablespoons barley malt & cocoa drink powder**
- **80g (3 oz) dessicated coconut**
- **80 g (3 oz) glacé cherries, halved**
- **1 egg, beaten**

Topping
- **280g (10 oz) sieved icing sugar**
- **55g (2 oz) butter or margarine**
- **2 tablespoons sieved custard powder**
- **boiling water – a little, to mix**
- **a little chocolate malt drink powder to sprinkle over topping**

Melt margarine, sugar and barley malt powder in a saucepan, or in a large bowl in the microwave.

Add coconut and cherries, mix well.

Add beaten egg, mix all and return to heat for a few minutes, stirring well as the egg cooks out (this works best in the microwave).

Stir in broken biscuits and spread mixture evenly into a swiss roll tin.

Cream together margarine, icing sugar, custard powder and a little boiling water to bind.

Spread topping over biscuit base, mark lines across with a fork , and sprinkle or sieve a little chocolate malt powder over topping. Cut into squares when set.

180. Date Slices

- **110g (4 oz) flaked oats**
- **110g (4 oz) plain flour**
- **110g (4 oz) butter**
- **55g (2 oz) soft brown sugar**
- **1/2 teaspoon bicarbonate of soda**

Date Filling
- **225g (8 oz) dates**
- **55g (2 oz) sugar**
- **a little water**

Grease a 20 cm / 8 inch square cake tin. Preheat the oven to 350F / 180C / Gas Mark 4.

Chop the dates and put in a saucepan with the sugar and a little water. Simmer until soft, mixing together to a spreadable soft paste. Set aside.

Put flour, oats, brown sugar and bicrbonate of soda in a bowl. Rub in the butter to resemble fine breadcrumbs. Scatter half the mixture evenly across base of tin and press down well. Spread date filling evenly across base mixture. Cover with the remaining crumb mixture. Bake for 30 - 40 minutes. When cool cut into slices.

181. Gur or Chester Cake

Traditional Irish baker's pastry, using up whatever was to hand. These squares very much varied from one baker's shop to the next, as their taste depended on whether the baker added in a rich fruit cake that had just dried out a little too much, or crumbled in a light sponge or flan case that had went out of shape in the oven.

- **225g (8 oz) ready-made shortcrust pastry**
- **110g (4 oz) plain flour**
- **3 teaspoons baking powder**
- **225g (8 oz) dry cake, crumbled finely - fruit cake or any type of plain cake is fine**
- **170g (6 oz) treacle or golden syrup**
- **a handful of currants, raisins and sultanas**
- **1 teaspoon ground ginger**
- **¼ teaspoon ground cinnamon**
- **¼ teaspoon ground cloves**
- **1 egg, beaten**
- **2 tablespoon milk or black tea**
- **a few drops of browning if desired**

Preheat the oven to 400F / 200C / Gas Mark 6.

Line the bottom of a deep swiss roll tin with the pastry, leaving sufficient for a lid. Sieve the flour and baking powder. Add the cake crumbs, dried fruit and spices. Mix with treacle or golden syrup and milk or black tea as required to make a rather stiff paste. If a darker filling is required, carefully add a drop or two of browning, mixing in well. Spread the mixture evenly over the pastry and cover with the remaining pastry. Brush with beaten egg and milk. Bake for about 20 minutesuntil the pastry is golden. Remove from the oven, sprinkle with caster sugar and mark into squares.

182. Red Currant Fudge

- **450g (1 lb) caster sugar**
- **400g (14 oz) double cream**
- **55g (2 oz) butter**
- **1 tablespoon glucose syrup**
- **1 rounded tablespoon homemade red currant jelly**
- **½ teaspoon raspberry essence**
- **a pinch of salt**

Line a 20 x 20cm cake tin with greaseproof paper. Put the sugar, cream, butter and glucose syrup into a saucepan.
Dissolve the sugar and melt the butter.
Bring the syrup to a steady boil, until the mixture reaches 116C or soft ball stage. Remove from the heat and leave to sit, undisturbed, for 5 mins, until the temperature drops to 110C. Stir in the red currant jelly, raspberry essence, and a pinch of salt.
Beat the mixture vigourously with a wooden spoon, until the temperature cools to about 60C and the fudge has become thick.
Pour the fudge into prepared tin and smooth over. Leave to cool at room temperature overnight. Cut into pieces the next day.

Irish Soft Drinks

183. Almond or Hazelnut Milk

Almond and hazelnut milks have been around in Ireland for some time, but are enjoying renewed popularity, with commercial varieties available in many supermarkets today. Both tastes great in tea or coffee, don't curdle like soy milk has the tendency to, and are lovely on breakfast cereal too. Just treat as ordinary milk shelf life in fridge and only make as much as you need for 2 or 3 days at a time.

(use any size cup as long as you use the same cup to measure the water)

- **1 cup almonds or hazelnuts**
- **1 cup warm water**
- **a pinch of salt**
- **1/2 teaspoon vanilla extract**
- **a little honey if sweet milk is desired**
- **more water**

Soak the nuts in water for up to 24 hours, then drain and discard the soaking water. Blend the drained nuts with the warm water on high speed for 2 minutes or so, until the mixture is so creamy that when you rub add a little of it between your finger and thumb you can feel no grit. Add a pinch of salt, vanilla extract, a little honey if liked, and 2 to 3 more cups of cold water. Cover the blender and whizz together for a few more seconds. If you find there is still any grit left in the milk at this stage, pass milk through a very fine strainer or muslin cloth. Chill and refrigerate.

184. Strawberry Crush

- **150 ml strawberry puree made from fresh ripe red Irish strawberries**
- **600 ml milk**
- **sieved icing sugar to taste**
- **vanilla ice cream**

Blend the strawberry puree together and sweeten to taste with icing sugar, Chill and serve with a scoop of vanilla ice cream.

185. Bramble Cordial

- **4 x 2 litre jugs full of ripe blackberries**
- **1900 ml cold water**
- **1.8 kg (4 lb) sugar (approximately - follow weights in method below)**
- **plenty of vanilla extract**

Pick over and wash the berries. Place in a preserving pan, cover with the water and let boil thoroughly until soft.

Strain well. Measure juice, and to every 950 mls of juice allow 430g sugar and 4 tablespoons of vanilla extract, (setting aside the vanilla extract until after simmering). Simmer for about 20 minutes. Remove scum and stir in the vanilla extract. Pour into hot sterilised jars and bottles and seal. Serve diluted with ice cold spring water.

186. Blackberry Shake

- **85 g (3 oz) blackberries**
- **280 ml (1/2 pint) milk**
- **2 tablespoons natural yoghurt**
- **35 g (2 heaped tablespoons) vanilla ice cream**
- **a little vanilla essence according to taste**

Wash the blackberries and push through a sieve to extract as much juice as possible. Add the rest of the ingredients and whisk together until frothy.

187. Oatmeal Gruel

- **2 x 15 ml level tablespoons oatmeal**
- **280 ml (1/2 pint) milk, a little more to dilute gruel if liked**
- **a pinch of salt**

Mix the oatmeal and milk in a bowl, cover, and leave for 30 minutes, stirring now and again. Sieve into a small saucepan, pressing out the milk, add a pinch of salt and bring to the boil. Simmer for 10 minutes, adding a little more milk if a thin gruel is preferred. Serve hot.

188. Barley Water

- **55g (2 oz) pearl barley**
- **peel of 1/2 lemon**
- **3 teaspoons sugar**
- **560 ml (1 pint) boiling water**

Put barley in a small saucepan and cover with cold water. Bring to the boil and boil for about 3 minutes. Strain barley and put in a jug with sugar, lemon peel and boiling water. Cover and let stand until cold. Strain. Serve plain, or add lemon juice and sugar to taste, or dilute half and half with milk.

189. Blackcurrant Tea

- **2 tablespoons home-made blackcurrant jam**
- **560 ml (1 Imperial pint) water**

Put the jam into a small saucepan, add the water, and simmer gently for about 10 minutes. Remove from the heat, sieve, and serve hot or cold.

190. Rose Syrup

Irish country gardens had beautiful rambling roses untouched by modern sprays or traffic fumes. Use only pure, natural, homegrown roses to make this Rose Syrup. In Ireland homemade Rose Syrup was said to be good with spirits such as gin (more likely mountain dew) and hot water for a cold; it's also beautiful as a flavouring in baking.

- **about 3 dozen roses – this will give you around 200 petals**
- **1.1 litres (2 pints) water**
- **450g (1 lb) sugar**

Cut the little white point from each rose petal, as if left in this will make the syrup bitter. Boil the water and sugar together for two minutes. Add all the rose petals and simmer on a low heat for 30 minutes. Leave to stand overnight. The next morning simmer again on a low heat for 15 minutes. Sieve the syrup and store in small bottles in the fridge.

191. Irish Moss (Carrageen) Lemonade

- a small handful of Irish Carrageen Moss
- 475 ml boiling water
- juice of a lemon
- 70 g (2.5 oz) sugar

Wash the Irish Carrageen well, cover with cold water and soak until soft. Pick over and wash again, add the boiling water and cook in a double boiler for 20 minutes until dissolved. Strain, add lemon juice and sugar to sweeten.

192. Apple Water

- 2 Bramley apples
- 560 ml (1 pint) boiling water
- juice of 1/2 a lemon
- sugar or glucose to sweeten

Wash the Bramley apples but do not peel them. Slice thinly, add sugar or glucose and lemon juice; cover with the boiled water and leave until cold. Sieve and drink. Serve warm as a soothing drink for colds and sore throats.

193. Donegal Carrageen Moss Drink
This drink was popular as a nightcap in Ireland, and considered "soothing to the stomach and chest."

- 280 ml (1/2 pint) milk
- 1 good sized sprig Irish carrageen moss
- a little freshly grated lemon rind
- approximately 1 rounded teaspoon sugar

Wash the Carrageen moss well until it is really soft. Put in a saucepan with the milk and lemon rind. Bring slowly to the boil, then simmer gently for 3 minutes. Sieve into a warmed cup, adding enough sugar to taste.

194. Irish Raspberry Syrup
Delicious with desserts and ice cream

Put as many **raspberries** as desired into a large bowl or bucket. Bruise them well with a wooden spoon or potato masher. Cover and leave for two days. Squeeze through a sieve, extracting as much juice as possible. To each 560 mls (1 pint) juice extracted, allow 225g (½ lb) **preserving sugar**. Melt slowly over a low heat, then simmer for 45 minutes. Remove any scum, then pour into warm bottles and cork.

195. Dandelion Punch

- **2.2 litre jug full of dandelion blossoms**
- **4.4 litres boiling water**
- **1300g (3 lb) sugar**
- **2 oranges**
- **1 lemon**

Pour the boiling water over the dandelion blossoms and let stand overnight- Slice the oranges and lemons thinly. Strain dandelion water, add sugar and bring to boiling point. Pour liquid over the oranges and lemons, cover and leave for 3 days. Strain before serving.

196. Elderflower Cordial

- **10 large elderflowers**
- **750g (1lb 10 oz) sugar**
- **28 g (1 oz) citric acid**
- **1 lemon**

Dissolve sugar in 560 ml (1 pint) boiling water. Stir in citric acid. Add grated zest of lemon. Slice the lemon but don't squeeze it. Add this with the elder-flower heads to the water. Press down and leave overnight.
Next day sieve all through muslin. Bottle and seal.
Serve diluted with chilled white lemonade.

197. Non -Alcoholic Irish Coffee

- **175 ml strong black coffee**
- **1 tablespoon Irish hazelnut syrup**
- **2 heaped tablespoons whipped cream**

Warm a coffee mug and add coffee and hazelnut syrup. Stir well, then carefully add cream so that it floats on top of the coffee.

198. Irish Berry Smoothie

- **140g (5 oz) fresh Irish raspberries**
- **140g (5 oz) fresh Irish strawberries, hulled and chopped in half**
- **2 fresh bananas, sliced**
- **400 ml natural yogurt**
- **ice cubes**
- **honey**

Combine all ingredients together in a blender. Whizz all together until smooth.

Irish Cocktails & Liqueurs

199. Sligo Slop

An old recipe from County Sligo (Spencer, 1913)

'This is an Irish delight.'

The juice of ten **lemons**, strained,
ten tablespoonfuls of **sifted sugar**,
one quart (1.1 litres) of **Ireland's best old whiskey**,
and two port wine-glassfuls of **curaçoa**,
all mixed together.

Let the mixture stand for a day or two, and then bottle. This should be drunk neat, in liqueur-glasses, and was said to be most effectual 'jumping-powder.'

200. Ratafia (Hannah Glasse, Dublin, 1742)

To every gallon (4.5 litres) of **brandy** put a quart (1.1 litres) of the best **orange flower water,** and a quart (1.1 litres) of good **French wine**; you must take care your brandy is extremely fine, and of a good age; put in **four hundred apricots stones,** and a pint and a quarter (up to the 700ml level in a measuring **jug) of white sugar candy**; just crack the stones, and put them in, with the shells, into a bottle; stop it very close, seal it down, and put it in the sun for six weeks; take it in every night, and in wet weather, and whenever you take it in, or set it out, shake it well about; after the time is expired, let it settle, and rack it off when it is perfectly fine.

201. Vintage Irish Cider Fruit Cup Recipe

- **diced fruits - apples, pears, skinned plums and blanched gooseberries**
- **egg white (buy eggs from hens which have been vaccinated for salmo nella)**
- **caster sugar, coloured green**
- **chilled Irish cider**
- **finger biscuits to serve**

Chill diced fruits well. Dip rim of serving glasses in a little egg white, then dip into coloured green caster sugar. Place selection of fruit in each glass, add chilled cider, and serve with finger biscuits.

Fast forward to the twenty-first century and Irish cocktails are still much in demand from bartenders in popular cocktail bars and salons around the world. The following recipes are some of the most well-known.

Please note:

Twenty-five millilitres or one fluid ounce (depending where you live in the world) cocktail measures like those used by professional bartenders are widely available for sale and not expensive to purchase. One measure in the next recipes is either of these single measures. If you haven't got your hands on either of these measures, 1 measure = 5 level teaspoons, or 2 x 15 ml tablespoons would work just fine.

202. Emerald Isle

- **2 measures / 4 tablespoons Gin**
- **2 teaspoons green Crème de Menthe**
- **3 dashes Angostura aromatic bitters**
- **1 green maraschino cherry**

Put first three ingredients in a shaker filled with ice and stir. Strain into a cocktail glass and garnish with the maraschino cherry.

203. The Irish Blackthorn

- **1 measure / 2 tablespoons Irish whiskey**
- **3 dashes Angostura aromatic bitters**
- **1 measure / 2 tablespoon dry vermouth**
- **3 dashes anise liqueur**

Combine all ingredients in a shaker with a little ice and stir well. Strain into a cocktail glass. Homemade Irish sloe gin is sometimes used in place of Irish whiskey in this drink.

204. Everybody's Irish

- **1.5 measures / 3 tablespoons Irish whiskey**
- **6 dashes green chartreuse**
- **3 dashes creme de menthe**

Combine all ingredients in a shaker with a little ice and stir well. Strain into a cocktail glass.

205. Irish Almond Cocktail

- **1.5 measures / 3 tablespoons Irish whiskey**
- **2.5 teaspoons / 1/2 fl. oz orange juice**
- **2.5 teaspoons / 1/2 fl. oz. lemon juice**
- **2 teaspoons Orgeat syrup**
- **1 teaspoon toasted almond slices**

Shake first four ingredients well with ice. Strain into a whiskey sour glass. Sprinkle toasted almond slices on top.

206. Irish Fix

- **1 teaspoon sugar**
- **2 teaspoons water**
- **2 measures / 4 tablespoons Irish whiskey**
- **1/2 measure /1 tablespoon fresh lemon juice**
- **1/2 slice orange**
- **1/2 slice lemon**
- **2 teaspoons Irish whiskey honey & herb liqueur**

Dissolve sugar in the water in a 215 ml / 8 oz. glass. Add whiskey and lemon juice and fill glass with crushed ice. Stir well. Garnish with orange and lemon slices. Float whiskey liqueur on top.

207. The Blarney Stone

- **1.5 measures / 3 tablespoons Irish whiskey**
- **1/2 teaspoon anise spirit**
- **1/2 teaspoon Curaçao liqueur**
- **1/2 teaspoon maraschino liqueur**
- **a dash of aromatic Angostura bitters**
- **a twist of orange peel**
- **a stoned green olive**

Shake first 5 ingredients together vigorously with a little ice. Strain into a cocktail glass. Decorate glass with the twist of orange peel and the green olive.

208. Irish Shillelagh

- 1.5 measures /3 tablespoons Irish whiskey
- 1/2 measure / 1 tablespoon homemade Irish sloe gin
- 1/2 measure / 1 tablespoon light rum
- 1 measure / 1 tablespoon fresh lemon juice
- 1 teaspoon superfine sugar
- 2 slices fresh peach, coarsely chopped
- 2 fresh raspberries
- 1 strawberry
- 1 cherry

Shake all ingredients except for the berries and cherry in a cocktail shaker with some crushed ice. Strain into a cocktail glass and garnish with the fruit.

209. The Tipperary Cocktail

- 1 measure / 2 tablespoons Irish whiskey
- 1 measure / 2 tablespoons sweet vermouth
- 1 measure / 2 tablespoons chartreuse

Stir well in a cocktail shaker with crushed ice. Strain into a cocktail glass.

210. Irish Cooler

- a swirl of lemon peel
- 3 measures/ 6 tablespoons Irish whiskey
- soda water

Put ice cubes into a highball glass. Add a swirl of lemon peel and whiskey. Top up with soda water.

211. Kerry Cooler

- **2 measures / 4 tablespoons Irish whiskey**
- **1/2 measure / 1 tablespoon homemade Irish sherry**
- **1 measure / 1 tablespoon orgeat syrup**
- **1 measure / 1 tablespoon fresh lemon juice**
- **iced soda water**
- **1 slice lemon**

Stir the first 4 ingredients in a tall glass with ice. Top up with soda and float the lemon slice on top.

212. Cold Irish Coffee

First make some iced coffee soda -
- **120 ml hot water**
- **2 tablespoons granulated sugar**
- **1 tablespoon instant coffee granules**
- **ice cubes**
- **80ml soda water, chilled**

Combine hot water, sugar and coffee granules in tall heatproof glass; stir until coffee is dissolved. Add ice cubes and stir in club soda.

To assemble the Cold Irish Coffee

- **1.5 measures / 3 tablespoons Irish whiskey**
- **2 teaspoons Irish whiskey honey & herb liqueur**
- **iced coffee soda (see above recipe)**
- **whipped cream**
- **1/2 measure / 1 tablespoon Crème de cacao**

Pour whiskey and whiskey liqueur into a tall 375 ml / 14 oz glass. Add an ice cube. Fill glass almost to the top with iced coffee soda. Stir. Flavour the whipped cream with the crème de cacao and add a large spoonful or two to the drink.

213. Retro 20th Century Hot Irish Coffee

- a tall heatproof serving glass filled to the brim with spring water
- 2 level teaspoons mellow powdered instant coffee
- 2 measures / 4 tablespoons of best Irish whiskey
- several heaped teaspoons of Demerara sugar, to taste
- chilled whipped or unwhipped very thick cream

Simmer water and sugar to make a light syrup. Remove from heat and add coffee. Warm a thick goblet or Irish coffee glass by rinsing it in very hot water. Pour coffee and whiskey into goblet. Top off to the brim with a generous spoonful of cream. Do not stir.

214. Irish Tea

- 1.5 measures /3 tablespoons Irish whiskey
- 240 ml freshly brewed hot Irish black tea
- 3 whole cloves
- 3 whole allspice
- 1 piece cinnamon stick
- 1 teaspoon sugar
- 2 teaspoons honey
- 1 slice lemon
- freshly grated nutmeg (optional)

Put whiskey, cloves, allspice, cinnamon, sugar, and honey into mug. Add freshly made hot tea. Stir well. Add lemon slice. Sprinkle with grated nutmeg if liked.

215. Misty Irish Cocktail

- 1 measure / 2 tablespoons Irish whiskey
- 1/2 measure / 1 tablespoon Irish whiskey honey & herb liqueur
- 1 measure / 2 tablespoons orange juice
- 1/2 measure/ 1 tablespoon lemon juice
- 1 teaspoon sugar
- 1/2 cup crushed ice
- 1 brandied cherry to decorate

Pour all ingredients and ice into a blender. Blend at high speed for 10 seconds. Pour into a glass. Add some ice cubes and the brandied cherry.

216. Mulled Beer

- 1 pint strong Irish beer
- 1/2 wineglass Irish whiskey
- sugar, ginger and nutmeg to flavour

Warm beer and whiskey until they cream. Flavour with sugar, ginger and nutmeg. Add a little cold beer to bring to the right temperature for drinking.

217. Hot Buttered Irish

- 1.5 measures / 3 tablespoons measures Irish whiskey
- 1/2 measure / 1 tablespoon fresh orange juice
- 1/2 measure/ 1 tablespoon fresh lemon juice
- 110 ml water
- 1 teaspoon sugar
- 2 dashes aromatic Angostura bitters
- 2 whole cloves
- 1 teaspoon unsalted butter
- 1 twist of lemon peel
- grated fresh nutmeg

Put first 7 ingredients into a small saucepan. Heat to boiling point, but do not boil. Pour into a preheated mug. Add butter and stir until butter melts. Add a twist of lemon peel to the mug. Sprinkle with grated nutmeg.

218. Hot Irish Whiskey & Port Drink

- 1.5 measures / 3 tablespoons Irish whiskey
- 3 measures/ 6 tablespoons port
- 2 measures / 4 tablespoons water
- 1 x 2.5 cm / 1 inch piece of cinnamon stick
- 1 slice orange

Pour whiskey, port, and water into saucepan. Heat to boiling point, but do not boil. Pour into mug. Add piece of cinnamon stick and orange slice. Leave to sit for about three minutes before serving.

219. Irish Alexander on the Rocks

- 1 tablespoon Irish whiskey
- 1 tablespoon Irish coffee liqueur
- 1 tablespoon heavy cream
- Ice

Shake all ingredients together with ice.
Pour into an antique glass.
Add ice cubes to top up glass to rim.
 Stir and serve.

220.Whiskey Honey

- 1 teaspoon honey
- A twist of lemon peel
- 4 tablespoons Irish whiskey
- Ice cubes

Put the honey in an antique glass with the ice cubes and lemon peel.
Add the whiskey and stir. Serve with a cocktail muddler for stirring.

221. Irish Shamrock

- **2 tablespoons Irish whiskey**
- **2 tablespoons dry vermouth**
- **3 dashes green chartreuse**
- **3 dashes crème de menthe**
- **1 green olive**

Stir liquid ingredients together well.
Strain into a cocktail glass. Serve decorated with a green olive.

222. Irish lemonade

- **3 tablespoons sherry**
- **4 tablespoons freshly squeezed lemon juice**
- **3 tablespoons sloe gin**
- **a twist of lemon peel**
- **2 tablespoons sugar**
- **chilled club soda**

Shake all ingredients except for the club soda and lemon peel together. Sieve into a tall glass, add lemon peel and fill up with soda.

223. Irish Cider Cup

- **1 litre sweet Irish cider**
- **1/2 teaspoon whole cloves**
- **55g (2 oz) sugar**
- **1/4 teaspoon whole allspice**
- **2 cinnamon sticks**

Put all ingredients in a saucepan and heat to boiling point.
Remove from heat and leave the spices to steep for 3 hours.
Strain, chill and serve with ice in glasses, or reheat and serve in warmed mugs.

224. Irish Apple Bowl

- **500 ml applejack**
- **500 ml Irish whiskey**
- **275 ml concentrated (dilutable) lime juice**
- **4 limes, sliced thinly**
- **2 large red apples**
- **2.5 litres ginger ale**
- **small block of frozen iced water**

Chill all ingredients separately in fridge.
Dice apples, leaving skin on.
Lay block of ice in a punch bowl.
Add all ingredients with the exception of the ginger ale, and stir well.
Chill in fridge for one hour.
Add ginger ale, stir well and serve.

225. Mc Brandy

- **3 tablespoons brandy**
- **2 tablespoons Irish apple juice**
- **1 teaspoon lemon juice**
- **1 slice lemon (to decorate)**
- **cocktail ice**

Shake all ingredients, except for the lemon slice, together well.
Strain into a cocktail glass. Garnish with lemon slice.

Irish Jams

226. Apple Clove Jam

- **1800g (4 lb) apples**
- **1700 g (3.75 lb) sugar**
- **700 ml / 1.25 pints) water**
- **2 level teaspoons tartaric or citric acid**
- **10 cloves**

Put water and tartaric or citric acid in a saucepan and peel core and slice the apples, throwing them straight into the saucepan as they are peeled. Add the cloves and cook gently until the apples are soft. Add the sugar and boil, stirring all the time until setting point is reached.

227. Strawberry & Gooseberry Jam

- **1345g (3 lb) strawberries**
- **675g (1.5 lb) gooseberries**
- **1800g (4 lb) sugar**

Wash and hull the strawberries. Wash and top and tail the gooseberries. Put the strawberries and gooseberries in a preserving pan over a very low heat. Simmer gently for about half an hour. Add the sugar, bring to the boil and boil briskly for about 10 minutes. Test for setting point. As soon as setting point is reached, pour immediately into hot sterilised jam jars.

228. Plum & Apple Jam

- **900g (2 lb) plums**
- **1350g (3 lb) windfall apples**
- **1800g (4 lb) sugar**

Peel, core and slice the apples and cook to a pulp over a very low heat, adding just enough water to prevent burning. Add the plums, with the kernels removed if you wish, though it is common to see a few plum kernels in pots of plum jam in Irish kitchens. Simmer until the plums are cooked. Add the sugar and stir until it is dissolved. Boil quickly for about 10 minutes, or until the jam sets when a little is placed on a cold plate. Pot as normal.

229. Raspberry & Redcurrant Jam

- **900g (2 lb) raspberries**
- **900g (2 lb) redcurrants**
- **1800g (4 lb) sugar**

Wash the redcurrants and remove any stalks. Wash the raspberries and put in a preserving pan with the redcurrants. Cook gently at first, then simmer for about 20 minutes, or until the fruit is thoroughly tender and the fruit mixture has reduced a little. Add the sugar and boil for five minutes. Test for setting point on a cold plate and pot as normal when ready.

230. Damson Jam

- **1800g (4 lb) damsons**
- **280 ml (½ pint) water**
- **1800g (4 lb) sugar**

Wash the fruit, remove all stalks and put in a preserving pan with the water. Simmer gently until the damsons are tender. Add the sugar, stirring until it dissolves, bring to the boil and boil rapidly for about 15 minutes. Test for setting point on a cold plate and pot when ready.

231. Rhubarb Jam

For every 450g / 1 pound of **rhubarb** allow 450g / 1 pound of **sugar** and 1 **lemon**. Finely shred the peel of the lemon into julienne strips. Squeeze the juice from the lemon and strain.

Put the sugar into a preserving pan with a little water, and bring to the boil. Skim frequently to clear of any scum that forms on the surface.

When it has reduced to a thick syrup, which on dropping a little into cold water becomes hard, add the peel and juice of the lemon.

Colour rather deeply with red food colouring and stir continually to prevent burning.

The jam will take about one hour's boiling. Test a little on a plate - it is ready when it sets sufficiently.

Pot in the usual way.

232. Rhubarb & Ginger Jam

- **2700g (6 lb) rhubarb**
- **2700g (6 lb) sugar**
- **85g (3 oz) bruised ginger**
- **rind and juice of two lemons**

Wash and chop the rhubarb and place in the preserving pan with the lemon juice and the bruised ginger and lemon rind tied in muslin. Bring slowly to the boil and boil until tender, stirring now and again. Add sugar and boil briskly for about 10 minutes. Test for setting point on a cold plate. When ready pot and seal as normal.

233. Rowan & Apple Jam (a 1944 recipe)

- **1075g (2.4 lb) rowans**
- **1075g (2.4 lb) apples**
- **2240 mls (4 pints water)**
- **4 lb sugar**

Pick over the berries and quarter the apples. Simmer with the water until mushy. Put through a sieve and then reboil for 30 minutes with the sugar.

234. Irish Blackcurrant Jam

Blackcurrants must be simmered gently in water first until the fruit is tender, in order to soften their tough skins. Then the excess water must be evaporated before the sugar is added. If the sugar is added before the blackcurrants are cooked, it causes the skin is to become tough and hard.

- **900 g (2 lb) blackcurrants**
- **840 ml (1.5 pints) water**
- **1.4 kg (3.25 lb) sugar**

Pick all the stalks from the blackcurrants, put them into a preserving pan with the water, and simmer gently until the fruit is tender, the contents of the preserving pan reduced, and the fruit thickened. Add the sugar, bring to the boil, and boil for 5 minutes or until setting point is reached. Pot in sterilised jars.

235. Sloe & Apple Jelly

- **1100g (2.5 lb) sloes**
- **650g (1.5 lb) Bramley or crab apples**
- **water and sugar – see instructions below**

Wash and prick the sloes and put in a saucepan with 560 ml (1 pint) water. Wash and chop up the apples roughly and put in a separate saucepan covered with 300 ml (0.55 pints) water. Simmer both until soft. Strain well, measure the juice; then mix both juices together and bring to the boil with 450g (1 lb) sugar to every 560 ml (1 pint) of juice. Bring to setting point and pot as normal.

236. Lemon Cheese for Tarts
Mrs. Gordon (1864)

- **900g (2 lb) butter**
- **900g (2 lb) pulverised sugar**
- **2 dozen eggs**
- **8 rough lemons**

'Have a brass kettle ready, put the butter and sugar in it and set it on the fire until they come to the boil. Then grate the lemons, and after squeeze the juice on the grated peel and pour into the butter and sugar. :Separate the eggs, yolks from the whites, and beat till light. Take the kettle off, and stir the yolks into the mixture when boiling and three-quarter part of the whites. Set on again, stirring briskly till it boils up two or three times. Put away in jam pots, and seal as with preserves.
N.B.-The only difficulty with the above is in stirring in the eggs quickly so as to prevent it curdling.'

237. Microwave Lemon & Rose Curd (a 1984 recipe)

- **110g (4 oz) butter or a firm good flavoured margarine**
- **3 large unwaxed lemons (should yield about 150 ml juice)**
- **2 teaspoons Irish Rose Syrup or essence of rose water**
- **225g (8 oz) sugar**
- **3 eggs**
- **1 egg yolk**

Grate the rind of the lemons finely, juice the lemons and put in a large microwaveable bowl with the butter. Cook on full power for 3 minutes. Add the sugar and rose water and stir in well. Cook for 2 more minutes on full power. Stir again. Whisk the eggs and egg yolk together well. Whisk through the lemon mixture and turn microwave to low power setting. Cook gently, uncovered for 12 to 14 minutes, in 3 minute bursts, stirring well in between each stage. The curd is ready when the mixture coats the back of a wooden spoon. Do not overcook. Pour into sterilised jars. Store in fridge for up to 2 weeks.

238. Blackberry Curd

- 170 g (6 oz) blackberries
- 55g (2 oz) Bramley apple
- 55g (2 oz) butter
- 1 lemon, juiced and the rind grated
- 225 g (8 oz) caster sugar
- 2 eggs

Peel and slice the apples and put in a suacepan with the well washed blackberries. Simmer until mushy. Sieve. Put in a double saucepan with the remaining ingredients. When the sugar has melted add well beaten eggs. Stir until thick and then pot in the usual way.

239. Rose Petal Jelly

- 450 g (1 lb) unsprayed damask rose petals
- 450g (1lb) sugar
- 4 tablespoons lemon juice
- 1.1 litres water

Prepare the rose petals and nip the white out of the base of each petal. Boil the sugar and water to syrup stage. Add the prepared rose petals and the lemon juice. Boil gently for half an hour.
Pour through a fine sieve, squeezing out all the juice from the petals with your hands. Return juice to saucepan and boil until the jelly reaches setting point.

240. Green Gooseberry Jelly

- 2.7 kg (6 lb) gooseberries
- 2.25 litres (4 imperial pints) water
- sugar

Top and tail the gooseberries and put in a saucepan with the water. Simmer until they are tender and broken up, then strain through a jelly cloth and weigh. Boil quickly for 15 minutes then add an equal quantity of sugar. Boil again until jelly reaches setting point.

241. Mint Jelly

serve with roast lamb

- **1350g (3 lb) apples**
- **2 lemons**
- **1700 ml (3 Imperial pints) water**
- **2 large bunches mint, well washed**
- **450 (1 lb) sugar to every 560 ml (1 Imperial pint) juice**
- **green food colouring**

Peel and slice apples. Put sliced apple in a preserving pan with the lemon juice, water and one bunch of the mint. Boil until mushy, remove the mint and strain apple mush through a jelly bag. Measure the juice and return to the pan, adding 450 (1 lb) sugar to every 560 ml (1 Imperial pint) juice. Simmer until the sugar has dissolved, then boil for 5 minutes. Dip the second bunch of mint in the pan, holding it in the jelly while simmer for a few minutes until the jelly is well flavoured. Remove the mint and boil until setting point is reached. Add a few drops of green colouring if desired. Pot in the usual way.

The Irish Bakeboard

242. Easy Oat Bread

Yeast-free, wheat-free and sugar-free, this wholesome oat bread is hugely popular in health shops right across Ireland. Allow to sit for at least half an hour before cutting.

- **340 g (12 oz) pinhead oatmeal**
- **110 g (4 oz) porridge oats**
- **45 ml (3 tablespoons) olive oil**
- **2 rounded teaspoons bicarbonate of soda / bread soda**
- **1 rounded teaspoon cream of tartar**
- **1 level teaspoon salt**
- **1 egg, lightly beaten**
- **450 g (1 lb) natural yoghurt**

Put oats, oatmeal, and sieved bicarbonate of soda, cream of tartar and salt in a large bowl. Mix together. Add yoghurt, combine all and let stand for 15 minutes. Preheat oven to 220C/ 425F/ Gas Mark 7. Grease and flour a 900g / 2 lb loaf tin.
After mixture has stood for 15 minutes, add olive oil and egg and mix well. Put mixture in loaf tin, level out and sprinkle a little porridge oats over top if liked. Bake for 20 minutes, then reduce heat to 200C /400F /Gas Mark 6 and bake for another 30 - 40 minutes or so or until baked through. Remove from oven, wrap in a tea towel and set on a cooling tray to steam out.

In Donn Byrne's fictionalised biography (1924) of Ireland's renowned blind bard Raftery, Byrne describes Raftery and his wife riding through the Irish countryside passing lakes, rivers, meadows and mountains,

'And they passed Kooig Meela Free, which is Five Miles of Heather, and there is a silken wind blowing over that townland, blowing the honeyed scent of the purple heather to the homesick people over all the world.... And they passed the townland of Kranna Arigid, Silver Trees, where the breeze keeps the leaves of birch and hazel in a shimmer, so that in the moonlight you would have good reason for thinking you had come to Tir nan Og. And the clusters of hazel-nuts in Kranna Arigid are the largest and richest in all the Irish nation, brown clusters in small green fronds.'

It was very likely Silver Grove Townland, Inchigeelagh in County Cork which Byrne was thinking of here. It's woodlands are rich in Seesile Oak, Hazel and Holly and nearby white clover and ling heather succour lovely local honey.

243. Silver Grove Brown Soda Bread

- **450g (1 lb) wholemeal self- raising flour**
- **85 g (3 oz) hazelnuts, walnuts & almonds, halved**
- **1 heaped dessertspoon Irish heather honey**
- **425mls (just over 3/4 pint) buttermilk, to make a soft dough**
- **1 rounded teaspoon bicarbonate of soda / bread soda, sieved**
- **30 ml (2 tablespoons) extra virgin olive oil**

Preheat oven to 200 C / 400 F / Gas Mark 6. Combine all ingredients together. Transfer to a greased and floured 2 lb (246mm x 146mm x 70mm) non-stick loaf tin. Bake for 10 minutes then reduce oven temperature to 170 C / 325 F / Gas Mark 3 and bake for a further 35 minutes or so until baked through. Remove from tin, wrap in a clean tea towel and set on a cooling tray. Remove tea towel after about 15 minutes and continue to cool.

Potato Bread, or Spud Bread, is a flat bread which originates in Northern Ireland, and is hugely popular on breakfast menus. It's served hot, fried with sausages, bacon, and tomatoes and tastes wonderful under a fried egg. Even roadside chippys serve up potato bread with the traditional Ulster fry. This recipe can be made without bacon; it's good just plain, or try adding chopped spring onions (scallions) to the dough.

244. Irish Potato Bread with Bacon

- **225 g (8 oz) warm boiled potato, mashed, seasoned and riced**
- **2 x 15 ml tablespoons melted butter**
- **enough plain flour to bind - approximately 28 - 55g (1-2 oz)**
- **approx. 55g (2 oz) cooked bacon, cut up as small as possible**

Place warm potatoes and bacon in a bowl, add butter, and sift in enough flour to bind to a dough. Knead lightly on a worktop dusted with flour. Roll out to about 0.6 cm / 1/4 of an inch. Place a plate on top and cut around the circle. Mark into quarter pieces. Dry fry very slowly on a low heat in a heavy based pan or a griddle – there is no need for any oil as the butter in the dough is enough.

245. Old Dublin Pancakes Recipe

- **4 egg yolks**
- **2 egg whites**
- **140 ml (1/4 pint) cream, warmed gently**
- **grated nutmeg**
- **sugar to taste**
- **40 g (1.5 oz) butter**
- **140 g (5 oz) plain flour**

Beat the egg yolks and whites. Mix with the warmed cream, add grated nutmeg and sugar to taste. Melt the butter gently and stir in the cream. Mix in the flour until smooth. Grease a low to medium heated griddle or heavy pan and drop batter to form pancake size required, turning when golden.

246. Soft Irish Brown Soda Bread / Wheaten Bread

Traditional Irish 'cakes' of soda bread were big, wide and oval shaped, baked in a large tin like those used to cook a turkey in at Christmas. This recipe uses equal quantities of plain and wholemeal flour. Many wheaten recipes are 75% wholemeal, giving a coarser bread. This recipe is much softer. A fine line like a crossroads was marked down the middle of the dough so that the large "cake of bread" could be divided into 4 quarters, or "farls" when cooled. When sliced, each farl has an edge that is crust free. As soon as the bread was taken from the oven, it was wrapped in a clean tea towel and set on a cooling wire. This is a vital final step in the making of the perfect brown soda bread. My maternal Great-Grandmother Mary-Ann was known to set her bread high up in the branches of a tree to cool it quicker. 15 children meant she had 'hardly time to bless herself', as my Granda used to say.

- **280g (10 oz) fine wholemeal flour**
- **280g (10 oz) plain flour**
- **1 rounded teaspoon salt**
- **1.5 rounded teaspoons bicarbonate of soda / bread soda**
- **70 g (2.5 oz) soft margarine**
- **55 g (2 oz) caster sugar**
- **420 – 560ml (3/4 – 1 pint) buttermilk**

Preheat oven to 220C / 425F / Gas Mark 7. Grease and lightly flour a large roasting tin.

Put the flours, salt, bicarbonate of soda and caster sugar in a large bowl. Mix together, then gently rub in the soft margarine, dispersing throughout the flour. Mix in enough buttermilk to make a soft dough. Do not over mix. Sprinkle worktop with flour. Set the dough out onto it and form into an oval shape, teasing and kneading the dough with the heel of your hand for a few seconds. Granny would toss the bread in the air from one hand to the other, kneading gently with this motion. Transfer to tin and mark a horizontal and vertical line across the middle of the bread like a crossroads. Put a small ovenproof dish half full of water on lower shelf of oven. Set bread in oven, reducing heat to 200C /400F / Gas Mark 6 after 10 minutes. After a further 10 minutes, reduce heat again to 180C / 350F / Gas Mark 4.

Check after about 35 - 45 minutes in the oven -the bread should sound hollow when tapped and a skewer inserted into the centre should come out clean. Remove from oven and wrap in a clean tea towel to steam the bread out and soften the crust. Set wrapped bread on a wire tray to cool.

247. Grandmother's Pancakes

The heavier the pan you use, the better; cast iron or heavy bakestones work best.

- 225 g (8 oz) plain flour
- 55g (2 oz) butter or margarine
- 55g (2 oz) caster sugar
- 1/2 level teaspoon bicarbonate of soda / bread soda
- 1 level teaspoon baking powder
- a pinch of salt
- 1 egg
- 280 ml (approximately 1/2 pint) buttermilk
- apples - a fresh slice for each pancake (optional)

Sieve dry ingredients and rub in margarine. Drop in egg and a little of the buttermilk. Mix quickly to a smooth paste and add enough buttermilk to make a thick batter.

Grease a low to medium heated griddle or heavy pan and drop batter to form pancake size required. Top each pancake with a slice of apple if liked. When base is set and bubbles rise, turn pancake and cook to a golden brown. Pancakes can be kept hot in a folded cloth while you finish making the batch.

248. Indian Meal Griddle Pancakes

- 70g (2.5 oz) yellow meal /corn meal
- 1 tablespoon sugar
- ½ teaspoon salt
- 235 ml boiling water
- 175 ml cold milk
- 110g (4 oz) plain flour
- 2 rounded teaspoons baking powder
- 1 well beaten egg
- butter to grease griddle with

Mix cornmeal, sugar and salt in a basin. Pour in boiling water and mix until smooth. Leave to swell for a few minutes. Pour in cold milk and mix again. Allow mixture to cool, then stir in sieved flour and baking powder. Add beaten egg. Warm griddle and rub over with butter. Drop mixture in rounds and bake on a low to medium heat. Turn pancakes when bubbles appear on top.

249. Potato Pancake

- **225g (8 oz) cooked potatoes**
- **55g (2 oz) sausage meat**
- **milk to mix (if using ready-made mash no milk required)**
- **1 teaspoon mixed herbs**
- **1 teaspoon chopped fresh mint**
- **1 teaspoon chopped fresh parsley**
- **salt and pepper**
- **white cooking fat for frying**

Mash potatoes with sausage meat. Add salt and pepper, herbs, and milk to make a soft mixture. Heat a little cooking fat on pan. Spread potato mixture to cover the bottom of the pan. Fry till crisp and brown.

250. Boxty Pancakes

- **450 g (1 lb) cooked, mashed potatoes, put through a potato ricer**
- **450 g (1 lb) peeled raw potatoes**
- **450 g (1 lb) plain flour**
- **1 teaspoon salt**
- **1 teaspoon bicarbonate of soda / bread soda**
- **buttermilk to mix**

Peel the raw potatoes and grate them on to a linen tea towel. Squeeze well, collecting the liquid into a bowl, and leave aside. Mix the grated raw potatoes with the cooked mashed potatoes. Add in the reserved liquid starch which was drained from the grated raw potatoes and mix well. Sieve the flour with the salt and the bicarbonate of soda, then mix this into the potato mixture. Add enough buttermilk to form a dropping pancake consistency. Mix well together and leave to stand for about 10 minutes. Warm a heavy pan or griddle and fry the boxty pancakes in spoonfuls on the greased pan. Cook on both sides and serve with butter and sugar, or enjoy for breakfast with fried eggs and mushrooms.

251. Springhill Sultana Scones

- **340 g (12 oz) plain flour**
- **28g (1 oz) caster sugar**
- **1 beaten egg**
- **225 g (8 fl oz) soured cream**
- **140g (5 oz) sultanas**
- **1.5 level teaspoons baking powder**
- **1/8 teaspoon bicarbonate of soda / bread soda**
- **1/4 teaspoon salt**

Preheat oven to 190C/ 375F / Gas Mark 5. Grease and flour a baking tin. Mix the soured cream with the beaten egg. In a separate bowl, mix flour, sugar, baking powder, bicarbonate of soda and salt. Add sultanas and mix through. Next add the egg and soured cream mixture and mix lightly until you have a soft dough. Turn out onto a well-floured worktop and roll out lightly to about 1.75 inches / 4 cm high. Cut out into scone shapes, 5 for large scones, or about 10 for smaller scones. Transfer gently to prepared baking tin and put in oven. After 10 minutes reduce oven temperature to 180C / 350F / Gas Mark 4, and bake for a further 10 to 15 minutes.

252. Yogurt Scones

- **675g (1.5 lb) self raising soda bread flour**
- **170g (6 oz) margarine**
- **1 large egg**
- **170g (6 oz) caster sugar**
- **approx. 250g (9 oz) natural yogurt**

Rub margarine into flour until it resembles fine breadcrumbs (slice it into small cubes on a floured board first). Mix in sugar. Make a well in the centre and add yogurt and beaten egg. Roll out to 2 cm / 3/4 inch thick and cut with a scone cutter. Place on a floured baking sheet and bake in a hot oven 200C/ 400F/ Gas Mark 6 for about 15 minutes.

253. County Tyrone Wheaten Scones

- **280g (10 oz) medium wholemeal flour**
- **170g (6 oz) plain flour**
- **70g (2.5 oz) butter**
- **70g (2.5 oz) caster sugar**
- **1 level teaspoon salt**
- **1.5 level teaspoons bicarbonate of soda / bread soda**
- **approx 275mls (1/2 pint) buttermilk**

Preheat oven to 200 C / 400 F / Gas Mark 6.
Sieve salt and bicarbonate of soda into flours and mix through.
Lightly rub in margarine until the mixture resembles fine breadcrumbs. Mix in sugar. Add enough buttermilk to make a soft dough.
Roll out on a well-floured worktop. Cut with a fluted biscuit or scone cutter and place on a floured baking tray, fairly close together.
Bake for 10 – 15 minutes until baked through.
Cool on a wire tray.

254. Glencar Faery Scones

- **225 g (8 oz) self raising flour**
- **2 level teaspoons baking powder**
- **1/4 teaspoon salt**
- **1 tablespoon caster sugar**
- **1 egg, at room temperature**
- **280 ml milk, at room temperature**

Preheat oven to 450F / 230C / Gas Mark 8. Thoroughly grease a 12 hole bun tin. Sieve the flour, baking powder, salt and sugar into a bowl. Beat the egg and milk together and mix into the flour mixture. Drop spoonfuls of the scone batter into the well-greased bun tins and bake for 10 – 15 minutes until well risen and just cooked through.

255. Griddle Scones

A traditional scone recipe using a heavy cast iron skillet pan, or a strong old fashioned bakestone type griddle - one of the handiest tools in an Irish kitchen.

'There were tea and hot griddle cakes for breakfast and there were fresh eggs; there was sunlight in the kitchen'
George Moore, Home Sickness (1903)

- **225g (8 oz) plain flour**
- **1/2 level teaspoon salt**
- **1 level teaspoon cream of tartar**
- **1/2 level teaspoon bicarbonate of soda / bread soda**
- **55g (2 oz) butter, margarine or lard (optional)**
- **just enough milk to mix to a soft dough**

Weigh out flour, salt, cream of tartar and bicarbonate of soda. Sieve all together into a bowl. If using margarine or fat, cut into little pieces and rub into the flour mixture until it resembles fine breadcrumbs. Mix to a soft dough with the milk. Roll out onto a floured board to a maximum depth of 1 cm /1/3 of an inch deep. Cut into rounds with a scone or biscuit cutter. Warm the griddle or cast iron pan. Grease lightly and cook scones for 5 minutes on one side, then turn over and cook for approximately 5 minutes on the other side until they are cooked through.
Don't have the griddle too hot otherwise they will burn on the outside before they are cooked in the middle. Serve warm with butter and homemade jam.

256. Breadcrumb Griddle Scones were made with a couple
of cups of **fine breadcrumbs**, mixed with an equal volume of **hot milk**. 2 tablespoons of **home-churned butter** was melted in, then half a cup of **flour** mixed with 3 good teaspoons **baking powder** and 1/2 a teaspoon of **salt** were stirred in. Finally, 2 well beaten **eggs** were blended in. Spoonfuls of this mixture were placed on a well buttered griddle, and baked until nicely browned on both sides.

257. Fluffy Light Potato Scones

Make sure your potatoes are well cooked, and then pass through a potato ricer to form a puree perfect for baking with. A food processor won't produce the same result as the starch in potato becomes glutinous when over processed.

- **280g (10 oz) self-raising flour**
- **2 level teaspoons baking powder**
- **1 level teaspoon salt**
- **55g (2 oz) sunflower margarine**
- **170g (6 oz) cooked, mashed potato**
- **up to 110 ml milk to mix**

Preheat the oven to 400 F/ 200 C/ Gas Mark 6. Grease and flour a baking tin. Sieve flour, baking powder and salt into a bowl. Rub in the sunflower margarine finely until it resembles fine breadcrumbs. Mix in the potato. Gradually add in the milk and mix to a smooth dough. Turn out on a floured worktop. Knead lightly for a few seconds and roll out to about ½ inch / 1.25 cm thick. Cut out scones with a fluted scone cutter and place slightly apart on baking tray. Bake for about 10 – 14 minutes until just cooked through.

258. Coconut Scones

If you are making a variety of scones and wish to identify the coconut ones easily, brush the unbaked scones with a little milk and dip in a fine dusting of caster sugar and desiccated coconut.

- **225g (8 oz) plain flour**
- **1 rounded teaspoon baking powder**
- **110g (4 oz) margarine**
- **70g (2.5 oz) caster sugar**
- **40g (1.5 oz) desiccated coconut**
- **1 egg, beaten**
- **milk to mix**
- **1/2 teaspoon vanilla essence**

Preheat oven to 200 C /400 F / Gas Mark 6. Sieve flour, baking powder and salt. Rub in margarine until mix resembles fine breadcrumbs. Add sugar and coconut and mix through. Add beaten egg, vanilla essence and enough milk to form a soft dough. Turn out onto a floured worktop. Roll out, dust lightly on top with flour, and cut into scones. Bake for approximately 15 minutes.

259. Rhubarb & Custard Scones

- 310g (11 oz) soda bread self-raising flour
- 2 level tablespoons custard powder
- 85g (3oz) sunflower margarine
- 1/2 large egg (about 27mls), beaten
- 110g (4 oz) Demerara sugar
- 200 ml rhubarb yogurt
- Small stick red rhubarb (55g / 2oz)

Wash and trim rhubarb stalk. Cut rhubarb once lengthways then chop into thin small pieces. Combine these in a microwaveable bowl with 2 dessert-spoons of the sugar. Microwave on high for 1 minute. Mix well and leave aside to cool.
Preheat oven to 200C / 400F / Gas Mark 6. Grease and flour a baking tin. Combine flour, sugar and custard powder in a separate bowl and rub in margarine. Add egg, rhubarb and yogurt and mix in lightly. Turn out onto a well floured worktop and roll / shape to a slab of just over an inch high. Cut out with a scone cutter and place fairly close together on baking tray. Bake for 12 to 15 minutes until just baked through. Cool on a wire tray.

260. Goat's Milk Wheaten Scones

- 155g (5.5 oz) medium wholemeal flour
- 85g (3 oz) plain flour
- 55 g (2 oz) sunflower margarine
- 40g (1.5 oz) Demerara sugar
- ½ level teaspoon salt
- 3/4 level teaspoon bicarbonate of soda / bread soda
- approx 135mls (1/4 pint) goat's milk, as needed to form a dough

Preheat oven to 200 C / 400 F / Gas Mark 6. Sieve salt and bicarbonate of soda into flours and sugar and mix through. Lightly rub in margarine until mix resembles fine breadcrumbs. Add in enough goat's milk to make a soft dough. Roll out on a well floured worktop. Cut with a fluted biscuit or scone cutter and place on a small floured baking tray, close together. Bake for 10 – 15 minutes until baked through. Cool on a wire tray.

261. Irish Restaurant Rich Wheaten Bread

Rich, full flavoured Irish Wheaten Bread, as served in pubs and restaurants across Ireland. Fantastic with seafood chowder, cheeses, homemade jam or marmalade.

- **225g (8 oz) medium wholemeal flour**
- **55g (2 oz) plain flour**
- **55g (2 oz) butter or margarine**
- **1 level teaspoon bicarbonate of soda / bread soda**
- **1/2 level teaspoon salt**
- **2 teaspoons golden syrup**
- **2 teaspoons dark soft brown sugar**
- **50 ml (just under 1/2 pint) buttermilk**

Sieve white flour, baking soda, salt and dark brown sugar into a bowl. Add wholemeal flour and mix well. Melt syrup and butter. Make a well and add melted syrup and butter, and buttermilk. Mix all together.
Pour in to a well-greased and floured 900g / 2 lb loaf tin. Bake at 375F / 190C / gas Mark 5 for 40 to 50 minutes until baked through. Remove from tin and wrap in a clean tea towel and place on a cooling rack. Remove tea towel after 20 minutes and finish cooling.

262. Praitie Oaten / Reusel / Potato Oaten Recipe

Quick and comforting ancient Irish recipe, similar to potato bread, but using oatmeal instead of flour.

- **170g (6 oz) warm cooked mashed potatoes, put through a ricer**
- **200g (7 oz) fine oatmeal**
- **pinch of salt**
- **approximately 2 tablespoons melted butter, or a mix of butter and cream**

Add enough of the fine oatmeal to the mashed potato to form a soft dough. Season with salt and melted butter, (with a little cream if liked) to bind. Sprinkle worktop with oatmeal. Roll the dough out into a 18 cm / 7 inch circle. Cut into 12 and bake on buttered griddle until lightly brown on each side.

263. Irish Treacle Bread

- **450g (1 lb) plain flour**
- **85g (3 oz) butter**
- **1 rounded teaspoon bicarbonate of soda / bread soda**
- **2 tablespoons treacle**
- **1/2 teaspoon salt**
- **1/2 -1 level teaspoon ground ginger according to taste**
- **up to 280ml (1/2 pint) buttermilk to mix**

Grease and flour a 900g / 2 lb non-stick loaf tin.
Preheat oven to 200C / 400F /Gas Mark 6.
Sieve the dry ingredients. Rub in butter (cut off into small pieces) into the dry ingredients, until all resembles fine breadcrumbs. Slightly melt treacle and mix well into half of the buttermilk. Add this to the rubbed in mixture and mix together. Add a little more of the buttermilk as needed to form a dough. Transfer dough to a well-floured worktop. Knead gently for a few seconds, transfer to tin, and put in preheated oven. After 20 minutes, reduce oven heat to 180C / 350F /Gas Mark 4.
Bake for another 15 – 25 minutes until cooked through.

264. Treacle Fadge Farls

- **170g (6 oz) plain flour**
- **1/2 level teaspoon salt**
- **1/2 level teaspoon bicarbonate of soda / bread soda**
- **1/2 rounded teaspoon ground ginger**
- **1 tablespoon caster sugar**
- **1 level tablespoon treacle**
- **enough buttermilk to make a soft dough**

Sieve the dry ingredients into a bowl. Slightly melt treacle with a little of the buttermilk and mix to a soft dough, adding more buttermilk as necessary. Turn out onto a floured worktop and shape into a round cake with a diameter of about 6 inches /15 cm. Warm the griddle to a low heat and grease lightly. Cut the dough into four quarters, or 'farls' as they are known as in Ireland. Transfer these to the griddle keeping them in the shape of a round cake with the straight inner sides barely touching each other. Cook very slowly for about 5 minutes, then carefully turn over and bake for a further 5 minutes or so until cooked through.

265. Buttermilk Oaten Bread

- 310g (11 oz) medium oatmeal
- 470 ml buttermilk or sour milk (+ extra if needed to bind next day)
- 280g (10 oz) plain flour
- 1 rounded teaspoon bicarbonate of soda / bread soda
- 1/2 level teaspoon salt

Steep oatmeal for about 6 hours, or overnight in the buttermilk.
Next day preheat oven to 400F /200C / Gas Mark 6. Mix flour, salt and bicarbonate of soda together. Stir in the steeped oatmeal. If necessary add a little more buttermilk, but keep the mixture stiff. Put on to a floured worktop and knead lightly until smooth. Roll out into a circle about 5 cm / 2 inches thick. Mark into four, cutting 2/3 way into the bread but do not cut right through. Ease pieces apart just a little. Set on a greased and floured baking tin and put in oven. After 5 minutes reduce oven to 375F /190C / Gas Mark 5. Bake for a total of 25 to 30 minutes. Wrap in a cloth and set on a cooling tray to allow bread to steam out.

266. Granny's Lightly Spiced Fruit Soda Bread

- 335g (12 oz) plain flour
- 110g (4 oz) butter or margarine
- 85g (3 oz) caster sugar
- 110g (4 oz) mixed dried fruit
- 1/2 teaspoon ground ginger
- 1/2 teaspoon ground cinnamon
- 1 rounded teaspoon bicarbonate of soda / bread soda
- 285 ml (1/2 pint) buttermilk

Preheat the oven to 190C / 375F / Gas Mark 5. Grease and flour a round cake tin 7 inch / 17.5 cm in diameter, 3 inch / 7.5 cm deep. Rub or cut in the butter or margarine into the flour to resemble fine breadcrumbs. Add the sugar, fruit and spices and mix well. Stir the bicarbonate of soda into the buttermilk to dissolve. Mix this into the dry ingredients. Spoon into tin and gently smooth evenly across top. Bake for 45 minutes, or until well cooked through. Remove from oven, wrap in a clean tea towel and set on a wire tray to cool.

267. Sultana Bran Soda Bread
A rich dark soda bread

- **55g (2 oz) bran**
- **3 x 15ml level tablespoons molasses**
- **475 ml buttermilk**
- **170g (6 oz) raisins or sultanas**
- **340g (12 oz) plain flour**
- **1 level teaspoon baking powder**
- **1 level teaspoon bicarbonate of soda / bread soda**
- **1/2 level teaspoon salt**

Grease and flour a 23 cm / 9 inch round springform cake tin. Preheat oven to 325F / 170C / Gas Mark 3. Soak bran, molasses, raisins and buttermilk in a bowl for 10 minutes or more. Sieve dry ingredients and add to bran mixture, mixing well to combine all together. Spoon into prepared tin. Bake for 45 – 60 minutes. Turn out onto cooling tray and wrap in a tea towel or baking paper until cool.

268. Malt Soda Bread

- **225 g (8 oz) self-raising flour**
- **1/2 teaspoon bicarbonate of soda**
- **1/4 teaspoon salt**
- **1 teaspoon dark brown sugar**
- **85g (3 oz) sultanas**
- **2 tablespoons golden syrup**
- **2 tablespoons malt extract**
- **140 ml milk**

Sieve flour, bicarbonate of soda and salt. Add sugar and sultanas. Add slightly heated syrup and malt extract to milk. Combine all ingredients together and mix well. Bake in well greased cake tin for 30 - 45 minutes 190C / 375F /Gas Mark 5.

269. Fadge Bread

There are all sorts of memories and descriptions of what fadge bread actually was. Stories abound of open air tea in the fields, with big plates of fadge bread thickly spread with homemade butter and smothered in homemade rhubarb jam. Most people's recollections of fadge bread are of a white or light yellow type of soda bread, either pot or brick oven baked, or fadge farls made on the griddle. This old fadge bread recipe has an egg added to give it a nice yellow colour. The dough is cut into 4 quarters or farls and baked on a griddle, or it can also be made into one round, baked, and then sliced in half to make the bases for two Paddy's pizzas.

- **225g (8 oz) plain flour**
- **1/2 rounded teaspoon salt**
- **1/2 rounded teaspoon bicarbonate of soda / bread soda**
- **1 egg lightly whipped with 30 ml (2 tablespoons) buttermilk**
- **more buttermilk (just enough to bind to a soft dough)**

Sieve flour, salt and bicarbonate of soda into a bowl. Mix in the egg beaten with the buttermilk, bring all together, then add just enough more buttermilk to bind to a soft dough. Do not over mix. Roll out the dough 1.25 cm / 1/2 inch thick. Cut it in 4 quarters / farls and set back in a circle, virtually touching each other on a warm, floured griddle, baking approximately10 minutes on one side and 10 on the other turning several times during the baking time. (Have the griddle, bakestone or heavy cast iron frying pan on a low heat. You can test this by sprinkling a little dusting of flour on it. It's the right temperature to bake on when the flour turns to an off white in a few minutes.) Set the fadge on to cook at this constant temperature until it has risen and a firm crust formed. When it's ready it will sound hollow when tapped and dry when split along the edge.

For yellow meal bread, substitute some of the wheatflour for cornmeal, using extra buttermilk if necessary.

270. Paddy's Pizzas with a Fadge / Soda Farl Base

For 2 pizza bases, follow Fadge Bread recipe, but roll the circle of dough out a little thinner and do not cut in 4. Bake gently on a floured griddle.

As soon as the bread is baked, slice it in half horizontally to give you 2 pizza bases. Add any pizza sauce and toppings you fancy; if they work for traditional pizzas they'll work just as good on a Paddy's Pizza. If you haven't time to make your own base, bakeries and supermarkets sell soda bread farls which work just as well and make preparation even quicker.

271. Lamb & Mint Paddy's Pizza

- **225g (8 oz) lean minced lamb**
- **1 onion, finely chopped**
- **30 ml (2 tablespoons) oil**
- **1 clove garlic, finely chopped**
- **1/2 teaspoon ground cumin**
- **1/2 teaspoon ground coriander**
- **pinch of ground cloves**
- **3 level teaspoons tomato puree**
- **200 g (7 oz) chopped tomatoes**
- **a little cheese if liked, and chopped fresh mint to garnish**

Fry onion and garlic in the oil, add rest of ingredients except mint, simmer until thickened and the mince is fully cooked through. Top base with mixture, sprinkle with cheese, bake or grill until bubbling, garnish with mint to serve.

272. Ulster Fry Paddy's Pizza

Cover base with **pizza topping or pasta sauce**, sprinkle with a little **cheese.** Arrange slices of cooked **Irish sausage**, cooked **Irish bacon** (chopped), **mushrooms** sautéed in **butter**, (chopped) a few **baked beans** if liked and a small lightly **fried egg** on top. Grill or bake until bubbling.

273. Irish Garden Paddy's Pizza

White Sauce
- **28g (1 oz) butter**
- **1 small onion, finely chopped**
- **28g (1 oz) plain flour**
- **235 ml milk**
- **salt & pepper**
- **a good pinch of nutmeg**

Melt butter, sauté onions in it, then add flour and cook out for 30 seconds. Add milk and seasonings and cook gently, stirring all the time until thickened. Spread over bases.

Topping Ingredients

Top with a handful of chopped **cooked vegetables** such as little cauliflower and broccoli florets, garden peas and small cubes of carrots (frozen mixed veg work well, just boil and drain before using). Sprinkle with grated **Gruyère cheese** and bake or grill until bubbling.

274. Buttermilk Point Picnic Loaf

*Just past the Loch gates, a little downstream from the island town of Enniskil-
len / Inis Ceithleann, lies the romantic Buttermilk Point. Legend has it that a
damsel stood at this beautiful point on Lough Erne selling buttermilk, inspiring
the passing boatmen to name it 'Buttermilk Point'. In 1938 the Enniskillen born
pianist Joan Trimble composed a fabulous reel of the same name, moved by
the beauty of the area around her. The waterway caressing Buttermilk Point is
dotted with islands, and locals and visitors alike enjoy picnics and cruising on
Lough Erne in fine weather. This local vintage picnic loaf recipe is a bit like an
ancient Irish version of the modern day tear & share bread. Enjoy it on its own
or slathered with cream cheese. The Bramley apple and sage are what give it it's
unique flavour.*

- 110 g (4oz) 4 rashers lean bacon or ham, cooked and finely chopped
- 1 large Bramley apple / about 225g (1/2 lb) peeled and chopped
- 1 medium onion, chopped
- 28g (1 oz) butter
- 1/2 rounded teaspoon dried sage
- 225 g (8 oz) plain flour
- 1/2 rounded teaspoon salt
- 1/2 rounded teaspoon bicarbonate of soda / bread soda
- 60 – 120 ml buttermilk
- 1 egg, lightly whipped
- cream cheese to serve

Preheat the oven to 375° F / 190°C / Gas Mark 5. Grease and flour a 900g /
2 lb loaf tin. Gently sauté the lightly cooked bacon, chopped apple, chopped
onion and butter together in a pan until apples and onion are tender. Allow
to cool. Sieve the flour, salt and bicarbonate of soda into a mixing bowl. Add
the cooled apple mixture and mix together with half the buttermilk and the
whipped egg. Add a little more buttermilk as needed to make a soft dough.
Transfer to the prepared tin and bake for about 40 minutes or until cooked
through. If the loaf is still a little light on top you can turn it over in the tin
and bake for a further 10 minutes or so. This is a well-known trick which Irish
bread bakers use, and is especially useful when baking in old style gas ovens
which don't have a fan. Serve sliced thinly, warm or cold, spread with a thick
layer of soft cream cheese, or fry in the pan the next day.

275. *Extra Rich Fruit Loaf Recipe*

Make sure all dry ingredients are at room temperature

- **225 g (8 oz) extra strong white bread flour**
- **1/2 level teaspoon salt**
- **1 rounded teaspoon vital wheat gluten**
- **28 g (1 oz) butter at room temperature**
- **28 g (1 oz) caster sugar**
- **1 egg, beaten (also needs to be at room temperature)**
- **125 ml warm water**
- **7g (1rounded teaspoon) active dried yeast**
- **335g (3/4 lb) partially rehydrated sultanas**
- **110g (4 oz) glace cherries (red and green are nice mixed)**
- **28g (1 oz) stem ginger in syrup, finely chopped**

Line the bottom of a 900g / 2lb / 23 x 13 x 7cm non-stick loaf tin with grease-proof paper and grease well with a little white cooking fat. Sieve the flour, vital wheat gluten and salt into a large mixing bowl, then rub in the butter until the mixture resembles fine breadcrumbs. Dissolve the yeast in the warm water and stir in one teaspoon of the sugar. Leave aside for 10 – 15 minutes until a froth is formed. Make a well in the centre of the flour, add remaining sugar and beaten egg along with the water and yeast mixture. Beat vigorously for about 10 minutes. Cover the dough and rest it for about 20 minutes in a warm place.
Add all the fruit to the dough and mix thoroughly.
Turn the dough out onto a well-floured worktop and knead for a few minutes, folding the sides and then the ends to the centre, until the dough is smooth. Transfer into the greased tin. Leave in a warm place until the loaf is well risen. In a very warm place this may take 1- 1.5 hours, in a cooler environment it could take overnight. Slow fermentation is just as good as rapid fermentation of dough.
Preheat oven to 180C / 350F / Gas Mark 4 just before the loaf is ready to bake. Bake in oven for 45 to 60 minutes, until a rich deep-brown colour and firm to the touch. When the loaf is cooked it will have slightly shrunk from the sides of the tin and sound hollow when tapped. Leave to cool before turning out of the tin, then finish cooling on a wire cooling rack.

276. Moist Irish Teabread

Teabread is probably one of the easiest Irish breads you could make. Some people pre-soak the fruit in stout, but Earl Grey Tea was an old favourite in my family. The oil of Bergamot in the Earl Grey Tea helps make this teabread taste extra special.

- **180 g (6.5 oz) mixed dried fruit**
- **160 mls strained black Earl Grey tea**
- **2 small to medium sized eggs, beaten**
- **110g (4 oz) light brown sugar**
- **140 g (5 oz) self-raising flour**
- **1/4 teaspoon mixed spice**

If mixed fruit contains peel, chop the peel up finely. Soak fruit in the tea for a few hours, or overnight.
Preheat the oven to 325F / 170 C / Gas mark 3. Grease and line a 900g / 2 lb loaf tin. Stir the beaten eggs into the fruit mixture, then add the sugar, flour and spice, and mix well. Put the mixture into the lined tin and spread out evenly. Bake for 45 – 60 minutes until cooked through.

277. Mrs Mulligan's Whiskey Tea Bread

- **450g (1 lb) mixed dried fruit**
- **140 ml / 1/4 imperial pint hot black tea**
- **30 ml / 2 tablespoons Irish whiskey**
- **225g / (8 oz) dark soft brown sugar**
- **225g (8 oz) self raising flour**
- **2 teaspoons mixed spice**
- **2 eggs**

Soak the frut in the hot black tea and whiskey overnight.
Next day preheat oven to 325F / 170C / Gas Mark 3. Grease and line a 900g / 2 lb loaf tin. Add sugar to the soaked fruit, then sieve in the flour and spice. Beat in the eggs. Transfer to tin and bake for 1 - 1.5 hours until springy to touch and baked through to centre. Cool on a wire tray.

278. Fast Food Savoury Pie Pastry

My hot food shop pastry recipe, perfect for filling with chicken, ham & white sauce, vegetarian curry pasties, individual steak & stout, minced beef & onion, potato, cheese & onion pies, or sausage rolls.

- 450g (1 lb) plain flour
- 170g (6 oz) white cooking fat
- 140 ml (5 oz) boiling water
- a pinch of salt
- a little whipped egg mixed with a little water (to glaze)

Add a pinch of salt to flour , then rub fat in until it resembles fine bread-crumbs. Add boiling water and mix together until bound. Roll out thinly on a well floured surface. Cut into 10 cm / 4 inch squares. Place filling of choice in middle of each square. Brush edges of square with whipped egg mixed with a little water (egg wash). Fold the squares over and seal edges using the back of a fork. Brush top of pastries with egg wash and make two slits to allow air to escape. Bake at 230C / 450F / Gas Mark 8 for about 20 minutes.

279. Stampy Bread – a type of Boxty

Typically served in the evenings in the fields at harvest time in Ireland. Some considered it quite indigestible unless washed down with copious amounts of whiskey, whilst others fondly remember it washed down with a big mug of cool milk or buttermilk. The name Stampy was probably derived from the method of mashing the potatoes. Try served with a hunk of Cheddar Cheese or smoth-ered in homemade strawberry jam on the day it's made. Save some for the next morning, slice thinly and fry on the pan and serve with bacon and egg.

- 450g (1lb) raw potatoes (peeled and grated on the fine side of the grater)
- 450g (1 lb) boiled potatoes
- 1 tablespoon buttermilk
- 55g (2 oz) room temperature country butter
- 450g (1 lb) self raising flour, sieved
- 2 rounded teaspoons bicarbonate of soda / bread soda
- 150ml soured cream
- 2 medium eggs (beaten with 2 tablespoons buttermilk)
- 2 rounded tablespoons caster sugar
- add a handful of caraway seeds if liked

Preheat oven to 175C / 350F / gas Mark 4. Put the warm boiled potatoes through a potato ricer to make smooth. Grease and flour, or line with grease-proof paper, two 900g / 2 lb cake tins, round or rectangular. Add the table-spoon of buttermilk and butter to the riced potatoes and mash well.
Mix all ingredients together and transfer to prepared tins. Bake for 60 to 75 minutes or until cooked through to centre.

280. Chewy Malt Raisin Bread

- **340g (12 oz) self raising flour**
- **2 tablespoons golden syrup**
- **2 tablespoons malt extract**
- **240 ml warm milk**
- **170g raisins**
- **a pinch of salt**

Line a loaf tin and preheat oven to 300F / 150C / Gas Mark2. Warm milk with syrup and malt extract. Stir in remaining ingredients. Transfer to tin, smooth over and bake slowly for about an hour or until cooked through.

281. Bramley Apple Scones

- **3 medium sized Bramley cooking apples**
- **a pinch of ground cinnamon (optional)**
- **450g (1 lb) plain flour**
- **1 teaspoon bicarbonate of soda**
- **a pinch of salt**
- **2 tablespoons caster sugar**
- **110g (4 oz) butter**
- **1 egg, beaten**
- **approximately 280 ml (1/2 imperial pint) buttermilk**

Preheat oven to 425F / 220C / Gas Mark 7. Line a scone tin. Peel, core and slice apples. Stew or microwave until soft. (Do not add any water). Add a pinch of ground cinnamon if liked. Sieve dry ingredients and rub in butter to resemble fine breadcrumbs. Fold in apples. Mix beaten egg with half the but-termilk and bind dough together, adding a little more buttermilk as needed to make a soft, but not sticky dough. Turn out onto a floured worktop and roll out to 2cm /3/4 inch thick. Cut into rounds with a large scone cutter. Bake for 20 - 25 minutes until cooked through.

282. Irish Stout Bread

- **275g (10 oz) wholemeal flour**
- **70g (2.5 oz) plain flour**
- **28g (1 oz) flaked oats, pinhead oatmeal, or wheatgerm**
- **1 teaspoon bicarbonate of soda**
- **1/2 teaspoon salt**
- **1 tablespoon demerara sugar**
- **28g (1 oz) butter or margarine**
- **1 tablespoon treacle**
- **100 ml Irish black stout**
- **approximately 200 ml buttermilk**

Preheat oven to 425F/ 220C/ Gas Mark 7 and grease and flour a 900g / 2lb loaf tin.

Put all dry ingredients into a bowl and rub in butter.

Pour in the stout, melted treacle, and enough buttermilk to form the consistency of very thick porridge or a soft dough.

Transfer the dough to tin and bake for first ten minutes at preheated temperature.

Reduce oven temperature to 180C /350F /Gas Mark 4. Bake for another 45 - 60 minutes or so until well cooked through. The base should sound hollow when tapped.

Remove from tin, wrap in a clean tea cloth and cool on a wire tray.

283. Tomato Bread

Perfect sliced with a big dollop of light soft cheese on top.

-
- **140g (5 oz) medium wholemeal flour**
- **110g (4 oz) plain flour**
- **55g (2 oz) soft margarine**
- **1 tablespoon caster sugar**
- **1/2 level teaspoon salt**
- **1 level teaspoon bicarbonate of soda**
- **up to a maximum 275mls (1/2 pint) buttermilk as needed to form a dough**
- **155g (5.5 oz) good quality fresh tomato salsa, drained**

Preheat oven to 200 C / 400 F / Gas Mark 6. Grease and flour a 450g /1 lb
non- stick loaf tin. Line the base of the tin with greaseproof paper.
Sieve salt and bicarbonate of soda into flours and mix through.
Lightly rub in margarine until it resembles fine breadcrumbs. Add sugar and
salsa and mix through.
Mix in enough buttermilk to make a soft dough.
Transfer to tin and level out top.
Put in middle shelf of preheated oven, reducing temperature a little after the
first 10 minutes.
Bake for 30 – 45 minutes until baked through.
Cool on a wire tray.

284. Cheddar Bread

- **500g (1 lb 2 oz) self-raising soda bread flour**
- **155g (5.5 oz) Cheddar cheese**
- **a pinch of salt**
- **500 ml buttermilk**

Preheat oven to 180 C / 350 F / Gas Mark 4.
Grease and flour a 900g / 2 lb / 23 x 13 x 7cm non stick loaf tin.
Combine flour, cheese and salt in a bowl.
Add the buttermilk and mix to form a soft dough. If the dough is too stiff add
a little more buttermilk.
Transfer to tin and bake for 50 minutes to 1 hour.

285. Yogurt & Banana Bread

Easy yogurt bread recipe. Pick your own favourite yogurt flavour to complement the banana.

- **120 mls natural / chocolate / coconut / hazelnut / pear / pineapple or vanilla yogurt**
- **200g (7 oz) plain flour**
- **1/2 teaspoon salt**
- **1 rounded teaspoon bicarbonate of soda**
- **1 ripe medium-sized banana**
- **a few tablespoons milk**

Grease and flour a 900g / 2 lb / 22 x 13 x 7 cm loaf tin. Preheat oven to 220C /425F / Gas Mark 7.
Warm milk, add bicarbonate of soda and stir to dissolve. Put flour, salt and bicarbonate of soda in a bowl. Mash banana well. Add the banana and the yoghurt to the dry ingredients. Mix all together, adding a little more milk if necessary to form a soft dough. Transfer mixture to loaf tin. Brush with a little milk to smooth out top of bread. Bake for 30 to 40 minutes until it sounds hollow to touch. Reduce oven temperature a little if bread is baking out too fast. Remove from tin, wrap in a clean tea towel, and leave on a wire tray to cool.

286. Shelled Hemp Soda Bread

- **350g (12 oz) self raising soda bread flour**
- **110g (4 oz) sunflower margarine**
- **55g (2 oz) Demerara sugar**
- **110g (4 oz) shelled hemp**
- **300 ml buttermilk**
- **1 rounded teaspoon bicarbonate of soda**

Preheat oven to 180 C / 350 F / Gas Mark 4. Rub margarine lightly into flour until it resembles fine breadcrumbs. Add shelled hemp and sugar and mix through. Stir bicarbonate of soda into buttermilk, mix well to disperse and add this to the dry ingredients. Mix together lightly. Transfer to a greased and floured 2lb / 900g loaf tin. Bake for 35 to 45 minutes until cooked through. Carefully remove from tin, wrap up in a clean tea towel and set on a wire tray, to steam out and cool down.

287. Savoury Pancakes

- 55g (2 oz) plain flour, sieved
- 285 mls milk
- 2 large eggs at room temperature
- good pinch mixed herbs
- rounded teaspoon chopped onion
- salt, pepper and chopped parsley
- butter or lard to fry

Make a batter with the flour, eggs and milk; then add the rest of the ingredients and allow to stand for at least half an hour.
Using a cast iron pan or hot griddle, fry in thin pancakes, and roll up. Fill as desired.

288. Spelt Bread

- 300g (11 oz) light spelt flour
- 200g (7 oz) rye flour
- 85g (3 oz) flaked oats
- 90 ml honey
- 330 ml warm water
- 2 g dry active yeast
- 3 level teaspoons baking powder
- 2 level teaspoons bicarbonate of soda
- 2 teaspoons salt
- 2 large eggs at room temperature, beaten
- flaked oats to sprinkle over top of loaf

Preheat oven to 325F / 170C / Gas Mark 3. Mix honey with warm water and sprinkle yeast over the mixture. Leave to stand for 10 minutes until a nice froth is formed. In a separate bowl combine spelt flour, rye flour, flaked oats, baking powder, bicarbonate of soda and salt. Slowly add the frothy honey mixture and beaten eggs to flour mixture, and mix until dry ingredients are well moistened. Place dough in 2 greased and floured loaf or cake tins and sprinkle with flaked oats. Bake at 325F for 60 minutes or until cooked through.

289. Scones Made With Cream

- **200g (7 oz) self-raising flour**
- **1/4 teaspoon salt**
- **55g (2 oz) caster sugar**
- **200 - 250ml double cream**

Preheat the oven to 220C / 425F /Gas Mark 7. Sieve the flour and salt together. Add the sugar and 200ml cream, then work in with a fork until you have even-sized-looking clumps. If the mix is too dry, add the remaining 50ml cream and mix through.

Transfer dough to a floured worktop and roll out 1cm / 1/3 inch thick. Cut out 5cm / 2 inch circles with a crimped scone cutter and place on a lightly floured baking tray. Bake for approximately 10 minutes, or until just cooked through.

290. Boiled Milk Scones

Delicious little bites; perfect with a soft boiled egg for breakfast.

- **1 cup or mugful of self raising flour**
- **the same cup or mugful of boiled milk**
- **1 teaspoon caster sugar**
- **28g (1 oz) soft butter**
- **a pinch of salt**

Put the flour, sugar, salt and butter in a bowl. Pour over the boiling milk and mix all together with a knife.

Turn out onto a floured worktop and knead lightly, adding as little flour as possible. Roll out very thin, cut into circles with a scone cutter, and cook on a well greased, hot griddle, turning once or twice during cooking time. Serve hot, buttered.

291. Cheese Muffins

Great with soup, make these into six large muffins, or smaller party size bites.

- **85g (3 oz) grated Cheddar cheese**
- **1/2 teaspoon cayenne pepper**
- **1 egg**
- **80 ml sunflower oil**
- **250 ml cup milk**
- **110g (4oz) plain flour**
- **3 rounded teaspoons baking powder**

Preheat oven to 190C / 375F / Gas Mark 5.
Mix egg and oil together. Add milk and mix again.
In a separate bowl sieve flour, baking powder and cayenne pepper together.
Mix in the grated cheese.
Stir into the liquid ingredients and mix together.
Spoon into well greased non stick muffin tins and bake for 20 minutes if muffins are large, a little less for small muffins.

292. Sophia's Soda Bread

- **450g (1 lb) plain flour**
- **1/4 teaspoon salt**
- **1 teaspoon sugar**
- **1 level teaspoon bicarbonate of soda / bread soda**
- **2 level teaspoons cream of tartar**
- **1 egg, beaten**
- **350 ml buttermilk**

Preheat oven to 350F / 180C / Gas Mark 4.
Sieve the dry ingredients, add the rest and mix well. Trasfer to a greased
and floured loaf tin and bake for approximately 35 minutes, until well baked
through.

293. Hot Cross Buns

- 600g (1lb 5 oz) strong flour
- 100g (3.5 oz) butter, at room temperature
- 100g (3.5 oz) sugar
- 300 ml warm milk
- 1 egg, at room temperature
- 9 g dry active yeast
- 1 teaspoon salt
- 170g (6 oz) juicy currants or raisins
- 28g (1 oz) very fine cut mixed peel
- 1/2 teaspoon freshly ground nutmeg
- 1/2 teaspoon ground cardamon
- zest of 1/2 an orange
- zest of 1/2 a lemon
- honey or golden syrup to glaze

Crossing Mixture for Hot Cross Buns

- 100g (3.5 oz) self raising flour
- 20 ml veg oil
- 110 ml milk

Dissolve the yeast in the warmed milk and 2 teaspoons of the sugar, and leave to form a froth. Put flour, rest of sugar, and salt into a large bowl and rub in butter finely. Whip the egg and add with the frothy milk mixture to the dough. Mix together and knead with a dough hook or by hand for about 7 minutes. Leave to rise until doubled in size.
Knock dough back and add the fruit, citrus zest and spice, working together well until evenly dispersed. Rest for 15 minutes. Divide into 70g (2.5 oz) pieces and mould into balls. Set onto an oven tray lined with baking paper. Allow to prove until doubled in size. When doubled , blend together the flour, vegetable oil and milk to form a smooth paste. Pipe on the crossing mixture in two lines along thr middle of the dough like a crossroads. Bake at 425F / 220C / Gas Mark 7 for 12 to 15 minutes. As soon as you take them from the oven, glaze with a fine mist of honey or golden syrup.

294. Bramley Apple Brack

- **225g (1/2 lb) Bramley cooking apples**
- **110g (4 oz) butter**
- **110 g (4 oz) sugar**
- **1 large egg, at room temperature**
- **110g (4 oz) juicy sultanas**
- **110g (4 oz) juicy raisins**
- **55g (2 oz) chopped walnuts**
- **55g (2 oz) chopped glace cherries (optional)**
- **170g (6 oz) plain flour**
- **1/2 teaspoon bicarbonate of soda**
- **1 teaspoon mixed spice**

Peel, core and chop the Bramley cooking apples. Gently stew with the sugar until soft, stir in the butter, and leave to cool.

Preheat oven to 300F / 150C / Gas Mark 3. Line a 900g / 2 lb loaf tin with greaseproof paper.

When apple mixture is cold, beat the egg and stir into the apples with the 1/2 teaspoon of bicarbonate of soda. Mix well. Sieve in the flour and spice and add the remaining ingredients. Transfer to tin and bake slowly for 1.5 - 2 hours until nicely baked through.

295. Donkey Lugs

- **300g (10.5 oz) strong flour**
- **50g (1.7 oz) butter, at room temperature**
- **50g (1.7 oz) sugar**
- **150 ml warm milk**
- **28 ml raw egg, whipped (1/2 a whipped egg)**
- **5 g dry active yeast**
- **1/2 teaspoon salt**

Filling:
- **homemade raspberry jam or jelly, sieved**
- **whipped fresh cream**
- **icing sugar to dust**

Dissolve the yeast in the warmed milk and 2 teaspoons of the sugar, and leave to form a froth. Put flour, rest of sugar, and salt into a large bowl and rub in butter finely. Whip the egg and add with the frothy milk mixture to the dough. Mix together and knead with a dough hook or by hand for about 7 minutes. Leave to rise until doubled in size.
Divide into 85g (3 oz) pieces and mould into balls. Set onto an oven tray lined with baking paper. Allow to prove until doubled in size. Bake at 425F / 220C / Gas Mark 7 for 12 to 15 minutes.
Set on a wire tray and leave to cool completely.

When cold make a cut vertically or horizontally and spread the opening with a little sieved raspberry jam or jelly. Fill with whipped cream and serve thickly dusted with sieved icing sugar.

Handy Tables of Weights and Measures

For precision, we have only rounded Imperial to metric conversions up or down by the slightest fractions. If you are using metric measurements we highly recommend that you use electronic scales. They are much cheaper to buy than they used to be and are the only way to ensure accuracy in your baking and cooking. You will find conversion tables in many popular cookbooks contain noticeable flaws in their calculations. It is particularly obvious where they calculate 10 oz as 275g and then calculate 12 oz as 350g. Small discrepancies really can make a difference with some ingredients.

Grams and Ounces Table

Ounces	Grams		fl oz	ml
1	28		1	28
2	55		2	55
3	85		3	85
4	110		4	115
5	140		5	140
6	170		6	170
7	200		7	200
8	225		8	225
9	250		9	250
10	280		10	280
11	310		11	310
12	340		12	340
13	365		13	365
14	390		14	390
15	420		15	420
16 / 1lb	450		16	450

1 teaspoon holds 5 mls
1 tablespoon holds 15 mls

Where teaspoons or tablespoons are stated in a recipe they are level, unless described otherwise.

Oven Temperatures

Ovens can be so temperamental that it really is worth purchasing an oven thermometer. They cost very little and could save you a fortune. It is surprising how some ovens fluctuate against the temperature on the actual setting knob and your oven may not actually be cooking at the temperature that you think.

Cool	275F / 140C / Gas Mark 1
	300F / 150C / Gas Mark 2
Very Moderate	325F / 170C / Gas Mark 3
Moderate –	350F / 180C / Gas Mark 4
Moderately Hot	375F / 190C / Gas Mark 5
	400F / 200C / Gas Mark 6
Hot	425F / 220C / Gas Mark 7
	450F / 230C / Gas Mark 8
Very Hot	475F / 240C / Gas Mark 9

Don't be afraid of your oven – long before the arrival of the modern oven, Irish bakers consistently managed to produce the most amazingly good breads on much more primitive heat sources. The secret is practice and getting to know when breads are just right, and just how much 'fire' or heat each recipe needs to cook it perfectly.

Conversions into American cups for American readers

1 American cup hold 236 millilitres of liquid. Other ingredients can be calculated as follows. 1 American cupful is a 236 ml measuring cup filled level or even with the ridge marked 1 cup. To measure dry ingredients such as flour, fill lightly with a spoon, taking care not to shake the cup. Level spoons or cups by first filling slightly heaped and then sliding the side of a knife across the top of the spoon or cup.

The following is a list of some equivalent measures which are all approximately equal to one American cup.

almonds, flaked, 110g (4 oz)
almonds, ground, 110g (4 oz)
almonds, whole, blanched, 155g (5.5 oz)
apples, peeled, cored and chopped, 135g (5 oz)
apricots, dried, 155g (5.5 oz)

barley, pearl, 200g (7 oz)
biscuit crumbs (digestive or Graham crackers), 110g (4oz)
blackberries, wild, 170g (6 oz)
bran, 70g (2.5 oz)
breadcrumbs, freshly made, 55g (2 oz)
butter or fat, 225 g (8 oz) 2 sticks
buttermilk, 236 ml

cayenne pepper, 110g (4 oz)
cheddar cheese, grated, 110g (4 oz)
cherries, glace, 170g (6 oz)
chocolate chips, 200g (7 oz)
coconut, dessicated, 85g (3 oz)
cornflour / cornstarch, 110g (4 oz)
cornmeal, 170g (6 oz)
cream cheese, 225g (8 oz)
currants, 170g (6 oz)

dates, chopped, 155g (5.5 oz)

flour, plain all-purpose, / self-raising, 110g (4 oz)
flour, coarse wholemeal, 120g (4.25 oz)

ginger, ground, 85g (3oz)

golden syrup, 350g (12.5 oz)

lentils, 200g, (7 oz)

mayonnaise, 250g (9 oz)
mustard seeds, 225g (8 oz)

nuts, chopped, 140g (5 oz)

oatmeal, medium, 200g (7 oz)
oatmeal, pinhead, 170g (6 oz)
oats, rolled, porridge oats 85g (3 oz)

peel, candied, 110g (4 oz)
pineapple, chunks, 210g (7.5 oz)
pineapple, crushed, undrained, 280g (10 oz)
pineapple, crushed, drained, 255g (9 oz)
potato, boiled and mashed, 225g (8 oz)

raisins, 170g (6 oz)
rice, ground, 155g (5.5 oz)
rice, long grain, uncooked, 200g (7 oz)
semolina, 170g (6 oz)
sultanas, 110g (4 oz)
sugar, Demerara, 205g (7.3 oz)
sugar, granulated or caster, 225g (8 oz)
sugar, icing, 125g (4.5 oz)
sugar, soft brown, 170g (6oz)

tapioca, seed pearl, 170g (6 oz)

wheatgerm, 110g (4 oz)

In Ireland and Britain a pint measures 568 mls. An American pint is smaller, measuring 473 mls. The measurements in this book are in millilitres but where pints are stated in brackets it is the Irish and British 568 ml pint which is meant and it has generally been rounded down to 560 mls.

Glossary

Aran hand knit cardigans and sweaters take their name from the set of islands where they originated many generations ago, off the West coast of Ireland. The Aran Islands lie at the mouth of Galway Bay, in the Atlantic Sea, a breath-taking landmark on The Wild Atlantic Way. Aran sweaters are made up of many combinations of stitches which can disclose vast amounts of information to those who know how to interpret them. Sweater patterns were closely guarded and kept within the same clan throughout generations. These Aran sweaters were often used to help identify bodies of fishermen washed up on the beach following an accident at sea. An official register of historic Aran patterns can be seen in the Aran Sweater Market on the Aran Islands. Aran knits are highly valued around the world today both for their originality and hardwearing durability.

Bakeboard - a large board usually about 60cm x 75 cm (2feet by 2.5 feet), kept specially for baking on. Dough was rolled out on, and bread kneaded on the bakeboard. The bakeboard was scrubbed clean and put away each day after use.

Bittern - A small bird in the heron family, now a red list species due to its small population and dependence on reed beds.

The **Blarney Stone** is world-famous for it's believed powers of giving you the gift of eloquence if you kiss it. It is built into the battlements of Blarney Castle in Blarney Village, about 8 kilometres Northwest from Cork city. Geologists have determined that the stone is made of local carboniferous limestone, about 330 million years old.

Botanic Avenue is 15 minutes from Belfast city centre, close to Botanic Gardens, the Ulster Museum and Queen's University.

Brawn - meat from a pig's or calf's head that is cooked and pressed in a pot with jelly.

Bread Soda - another name for bicarbonate of soda

Buttermilk was traditionally a by-product of butter-making, being the liquid that was left over after butter was churned from cream. It is now made commercially by adding a bacterial culture to skimmed milk.

Carrageen - A kind of seaweed (Chondrus crispus), also called Irish moss, common on the Irish coast. It has a cartilaginous texture and a purplish colour, becoming yellowish-white when dried. When boiled it is frequently used instead of gelatine for making blanc-mange and jelly. It was introduced into medical use by a Mr. Todhunter of Dublin. (Reece's Monthly Gazette of Health, Jan. 1831.)

Celtic Tiger - Nickname given to the Irish economy during its period of rapid growth in the 1990s and early 2000s.

Colleen - Anglo Irish word meaning a lass or a girl. Also a popular girls name.

Dariole Mould - a very small tin mould shaped like a flower pot.

Farl – a shape of bread made by marking a circular cake of bread with a deep cross, so that it can easily be broken into quarters or 'farls' after baking.

Goat Kid Meat is regaining popularity again and is more ethical than one might think. When goats are bred for Irish and British dairy farming, the male goats are usually killed at birth, as only females are kept for milk and cheese. Recently several goat farms have reversed this trend, successfully rescuing thousands of billy goat kids and reintroducing a meat to the menu which is low in fat and high in protein and iron.

Griddle – A round cast iron plate with a semi-circular handle which was traditionally placed over an open turf fire. A bake stone or heavy cast iron pan can also be used for recipes which call for a griddle.

Hiberno-English - The dialect of English often spoken in Northern Ireland and the Republic of Ireland takes much of its grammar and structure from the Irish language. One noticeable difference is that there is no 'have' in Irish. This is why instead of saying 'I have baked a cake', it is common to hear someone say, 'I'm after baking a cake'.

Irish Rosé Veal - Veal is the name of the light-coloured meat from young calves. It is widely eaten on the Continent and is commonly found on restaurant menus in France, Belgium and Italy. Thousands of Irish calves are exported to the Continent each year, many for veal production. Scientific studies have shown that young calves are poor travellers and are prone to becoming ill, particularly in the weeks following their journey. Veal rearing is normally indoors, with no access to outdoors, and this is permitted by EU law. There are humane veal systems in Ireland where groups of calves are kept indoors with natural light, plenty of straw and room to move around freely. The veal from these more welfare-friendly systems is usually called 'rosé veal', and is believed by many to be a much better alternative to exporting young Irish calves to the Continent.

Irish Sausages are very different from continental or hot dog style sausages. Irish sausages are made from ground pork, pork fat, rusk, potato starch and soya and flavoured with nutmeg and sage extracts. The everyday Irish sausage remains more popular than gourmet sausages which contain a higher meat content and don't have as smooth a taste.

Lobsters should be bought live, or ready cooked from a fishmonger. The reason for this is because their diet is full of toxins which cause the flesh to go off rapidly after the lobster dies.

Pinhead Oatmeal is made from whole oats that have been cut into two or three pieces by steel cutters to produce rough, coarse oatmeal. They are also known as steel-cut oats.

Potato Ricer - A kitchen utensil used for pressing mashed potatoes, giving a smooth lump-free result similar to sieving.

Ragout – a richly flavoured meat stew.

Rubbing in – The method of distributing a fat such as butter, margarine or lard through a dry mixture, usually flour, by rubbing with the thumb across the fingertips, until the whole mixture resembles fine breadcrumbs.

Sal Volatile - listed in some old Ulster recipe books, Sal Volatile was the name for ammonium carbonate, a raising agent which used to be used in baking cakes. It could also be purchased in an aromatic solution to be used as a restorative smelling salt in the treatment of fainting fits.

It is also known as baker's ammonia and was a predecessor to the more modern leavening agents baking soda and baking powder.

Scallions – another name for spring onions / green onions. Scallions grow well in Ireland and are a popular ingredient in fresh salads and in the iconic potato dish 'Colcannon'. When available they are often snipped into small pieces and mixed with simple mashed potatoes and a good knob of country butter.

Treacle is any uncrystallised syrup made during the refining of sugar. The most common forms of treacle are golden syrup, a pale variety, and a darker variety known as black treacle. Black treacle, or molasses, has a distinctively strong, slightly bitter flavour, and is a richer colour than golden syrup. For baking purposes, when an Irish recipe states 'treacle' it is generally referring to black treacle, or molasses.

Wheaten - Though generally wheaten refers to the colour of a loaf when baked with wholemeal flour, in Northern Ireland 'a wheaten' is a cake of brown soda bread.

Equivalents

bacon - back bacon - Canadian bacon
bacon rashers – bacon slices
baking tray - baking sheet
beef stock - brown stock
beetroot – beet
bicarbonate of soda - baking soda - bread soda
biscuits - cookies
brown sugar - Barbados sugar
caster sugar – super fine sugar
celery stick - celery rib
chop - cutlet
cornflour - cornstarch
Cornish pasty - meat turnover
Demerara sugar - raw sugar
digestive biscuits - Graham crackers
double cream - heavy cream
essence – extract
faery cake - cupcake
frying pan – skillet
golden syrup - dark cane sugar syrup
greaseproof paper - wax paper
hard-boiled eggs - hard-cooked eggs
hazelnuts - filberts
icing - frosting
icing sugar – confectioner's sugar / powdered sugar
Irish sausages - bangers
jelly - jello
liquidiser - blender
minced meat - ground meat
mixed spice - allspice

muslin – cheesecloth
natural yogurt – plain yogurt
plain flour – all purpose flour
prawns – shrimp
self raising flour - self rising flour
semolina - farina
shortcrust pastry – pie dough
stock cube - bouillon cube
strong flour - bread flour
whipping cream - heavy cream
spring onions – scallions – green onions
sultanas – golden raisins
tart - pie
tinned - canned
tomato purée -tomato paste
toffee - taffy
treacle – molasses
wholemeal flour – wholewheat flour

Buttermilk Substitute -

If you don't have any buttermilk you can make your own buttermilk substitute by mixing 240 mls of milk with a tablespoon of lemon juice or vinegar. Once mixed leave to stand for 5 minutes before using.

Acknowledgements

Thank you to close friends, family and all those whose family recipes have intermingled to lend character to this book. Thank you to Patricia Hey and her Mum Bettine Simpson for access to Patricia's grandmother's handwritten notebook. Thanks also to Patricia for tracking down recipes from other families' archives. Thank you to Dorothy Bruce for access to Jenny McKee's recipe notebooks, and to the Flynn family for access to Sarah Flynn's recipes. A special mention and thanks also to Josephine Batterham for kind permission to use her Uncle Derek Hill's recipes and to the Deputy Keeper of the Records, Public Record Office of Northern Ireland.

Bibliography & References

Byrne, D. (first published 1924) *Blind Raftery and his Wife, Hilaria* London: Sampson Low, Marston & Co.

Edgeworth, M. (1816) *Edgeworth's Works: Moral tales: v. 1. Forester, and The Prussian vase* R. Hunter and Baldwin, Cradock, and Joy (p.77)

Carmichael Ferrall, E. (1913) *The Augher Book of Maxims, Household Hints and Recipes* W.G. Baird, Belfast

Dono, V. (2014) *Dreams & Recipes 1904 – 1914* Analogy Press, Belfast

Glasse, H. (1742) *The Compleat Confectioner*, Dublin

Hyde, H.M. (1979) *The Londonderrys, a Family Portrait* Hamish Hamilton Ltd, London

Joyce, J. (1914) *Dubliners* Grant Richards, London

Kander, L.B. (undated) *The Way to a Man's Heart* The Settlement Cook Book Company

Moore, G. (1903) *The Untilled Field* T. Fisher Unwin, London

J. B. Lyons, 'Whitla, Sir William (1851–1933)', Oxford Dictionary of National Biography, Oxford University Press, 2004; online edn, Sept 2010 [http://www. oxforddnb.com/view/article/36874, accessed 15 Nov 2014]

PRONI, The Derek Hill archive D4400/D/5/17/A, D440/D/5/17/ 40 and 47

Q.C.B. Cookbook (1907) compiled in connection with Queens College Fête, Belfast

Spencer, E. (Nathaniel Gubbins) (1897, reprinted 1913) *Cakes & Ale, a dissertation on banquets interspersed with various recipes, more or less original, and anecdotes, mainly veracious* fourth edition Stanley Paul & Co.

The Irish Society Review September 24, 1904

Bibliography & References (continued)

Whelan, D. (2005) The Castle and Manor of Mocollop, Co. Waterford available online at http://snap.waterfordcoco.ie/collections/etheses/whelan_david/whelan_david_1.pdf (Accessed 22nd November 2014)

Index

Almond or Hazelnut Milk   125
Almond Rice Cream   91
Almond Slices   114
Almond Topped Gooseberry Pie   100
An Apple Hedgehog   58
Anraith an Lae - Soup of the Day   36
Apple & Blackberry Trifle, Hot   98
Apple Cheesecakes, Botanic   83
Apple Clove Jam   143
Apple Sponge Pudding   93
Apple Tart (thick pastry)   78
Apple Tart (really thin pastry)   77
Apple Water   128
Atlantic Coast Seafood Tian   27

Barley Water   127
Beef, Fillet of   44
Belfast Batch Bread Snacks   38
Berry Smoothie   130
Biscuit Fudge   118
Blackberries and Apple, Stewed   98
Blackberries, Next Day   95
Blackberry & Bramley Apple Autumn Pudding   96
Blackberry Curd   148
Blackberry Dessert Jelly   97
Blackberry Roll   97
Blackberry Shake   126
Blackberry Topping (for yogurt or cheesecake)   99
Blackcurrant & Bramley Apple Tart   76
Blackcurrant Jam   146
Blackcurrant Tea   127
Boiled Fruit Cake   79
Boiled Milk Scones   177
Boxty Pancakes   156
Bramble Cordial   126

Bramble Duff Pudding   95
Bramley Apple Brack   180
Bramley Apple Fool   94
Bramley Apple Gingerbread   82
Bramley Apple Meringue Pudding   92
Bramley Apple Scones   172
Bramloffee Pie   102
Brandy Butter   105
Breadcrumb Griddle Scones   159
Bride's Slices   116
Brown Sauce   64
Brown Soda Bread   69, 154
Brown Soda Bread, Silver Grove   152
Brown Stew   19
Buns, Mum's easy 3,4,5,6 Buns   86
Buttermilk Brack   68
Buttermilk Dumpling   106
Buttermilk Oaten Bread   164
Buttermilk Point Picnic Loaf   168

Cabbage in Butter   47
Cabbage, Tory Island   60
Celtic Tiger Shortbread   119
Champ, Scallion   49
Chapel Windows   120
Cheddar Bread   174
Cheese Muffins   178
Cherry Cakes   55
Chicken Omelette, Old Belfast Recipe   42
Chocolate Cake   81
Chocolate Faery Cakes   87
Chocolate Icing   81
Chocolate Peppermint Squares   118
Christmas Crumble   106
Christmas Plum Pudding in a Flash   104
Christmas Pudding   105
Cider Trout   45
Coconut Macaroon Tartlets   83
Coconut Scones   160
Cod Roes, Poached   41
Colcannon Mash, Creamy   20

Cold Irish Coffee   136
Cottage Potatoes   48
Crab Quiche, Donegal   32
Crab, Devilled   53
Craiceann   35
Curd, Microwave Lemon & Rose   147
Cú Chulainn Salmon   24

D amson Jam   144
Dandelion Punch   129
Date 'n' Walnut Cake   74
Date Slices   121
Donegal Carrageen Moss Drink   128
Donegal Pie Recipe   31
Donkey Lugs   181
Dublin Bacon Coddle   29

E el Pie, Lough Erne   30
Eggs Prince Congal   43
Eggs, scrambled with Irish Smoked Salmon   22
Elderflower Cordial   129
Emerald Isle   133
Emer's Sauce   25
Erin Cakes   88
Everybody's Irish   133

F adge Bread, Soda   166
Fadge Bread, Wheaten   57
Fifteens   114
Fillet Steak in a Bramble Jus   22
Fish Mould   33
Fish Steamed Between Two Plates   45
Florence Cake, Belfast   73
Fruit Compote   101
Fruit Loaf, Extra Rich   169

Fruit Soda Bread, Granny's Lightly Spiced   164
Fruit Squares, Mum's   112

Ginger Sponge Squares   116
Ginger Wine   66
Glencar Faery Scones   158
Gluten Free Yogurt Cake   80
Goat Kid Meat Stew   48
Goat's Milk Wheaten Scones   161
Gooseberry Chutney   64
Granny's Favourite Traybake   120
Green Gooseberry Jelly   148
Griddle Scones   159
Gur or Chester Cake   122

Ham Butter   51
Harvey's Sauce   31
Herring Log, Atlantic   39
Honey Cakes   87
Honeycomb   90
Honeycomb Cheesecake   89
Hot Buttered Irish   138
Hot Cross Buns   179
Hot Irish Whiskey & Port Drink   139
Hotch Potch, Irish   41

Indian Meal Griddle Pancakes Recipe   155
Irish Alexander on the Rocks   139
Irish Almond Cocktail   134
Irish Apple Bowl   141
Irish Berry Smoothie   130
Irish Bread & Butter Pudding   99
Irish Cider Cup   140
Irish Coffee Dessert Cake   109
Irish Coffee Jelly   110
Irish Coffee, cold   136
Irish Coffee, hot   137

Irish Coffee, non-alcoholic   130
Irish Cooler   135
Irish Fix   134
Irish Garden Paddy's Pizza   167
Irish Lemonade   140
Irish Moss (Carrageen) Lemonade   128
Irish Raspberry Syrup
Irish Shamrock   140
Irish Shillelagh   135
Irish Stew, Easy   19
Irish Tea   137
Ivory Cream Recipe   68

Jam Sauce for Plain Sponge Puddings   107

Kerry Apple Cake   74
Kerry Cooler   136

Lamb & Mint Paddy's Pizza   167
Lamb Chops, Grilled with Victoria Plums   52
Lamb Dinner by the Peat Turf Fire   21
Leitrim Brawn Recipe   34
Lemonade, Irish Moss (Carrageen)   128
Lemon Cheese for Tarts   147
Lemon Coconut Slices   117
Lemon & Rose Curd   147
Lentil Irish Stew   49
Limerick Ham, Baked in Cider   47
Lobster Cream   32
Lobster Sauce   25

Mallow Snowballs   117
Malt Raisin Bread   172
Malt Soda Bread   165
Marie's Bars   115

Marrow Dumplings for Soups & Broths   46
Marrow Marmalade   56
Marshmallow Crispy Squares   114
McBrandy   141
Meatloaf   40
Mint Choc Bubble Bar Cheesecake   91
Mint Jelly   149
Misty Irish Cocktail   138
Mixed Grill, Irish   18
Mulled Beer   138
Mutton, Ragout   50

Nettle & Oatmeal Broth   36
Nettle Stuffing   46
Non -Alcoholic Irish Coffee   130

Oat Bread   151
Oaten Apple Slice   113
Oaten Shortbread   119
Oatmeal Gruel   126
Orange & Blackberry Pudding   89

Paddy's Pizzas with a Fadge / Soda Farl Base   166
Pancakes Colleen   18
Pancakes, Grandmother's   155
Pancakes, Old Dublin   153
Paradise Squares   113
Parsley Butter   51
Parsley Honey   65
Pastie Recipe, Belfast Chip Shop   37
Pastry, Fast Food Savoury Pie   171
Pastry, Simple Irish Baker's Short Paste   76
Peas, Minted   51
Pheasant, Little Creams   45
Pheasant, Pan Seared Breast of   49
Picnic Loaf, savoury   168
Pineapple Boiled Fruit Cake   80

Pineapple Creams 84
Pineapple Delights 111
Plaice, Dun Laoghaire Fried 50
Plate Apple Tart (really thin pastry) 77
Plum & Apple Jam 144
Porter Cake 75
Potato Apple 103
Potato Bread with Bacon 153
Potato Pancake 156
Potato Pastry 69
Potato Pudding 104
Potato Scones 160
Praitie Oaten / Reusel / Potato Oaten Recipe 162
Prátaí Inis Ceithleann 39
Prawn Cocktail, Dublin Bay 28
Promisques 42

Rabbit, Galantine of 44
Rarebit, Dublin 28
Raspberry & Redcurrant Jam 144
Raspberry Syrup 129
Ratafia 132
Redcurrant Fudge 123
Redcurrant Bread & Butter Pudding 108
Reusel 162
Rhubarb & Custard Scones 161
Rhubarb & Ginger Jam 145
Rhubarb Crumble 102
Rhubarb Jam 145
Rhubarb or Gooseberry Chutney 64
Rhubarb, Steamed 94
Rice with Plums 101
Rich Wheaten Bread, Irish Restaurant 162
Rissoles 65
Rock Buns 85
Rose Fondant Icing 81
Rose Petal Jelly 148
Rose Syrup 127
Rowan & Apple Jam (a 1944 recipe) 145

Sago Pudding with Bramble Jelly   108
Salad Dressing, Gracie's   61
Salmon Bisque, Gracie McDermott's   61
Salmon Fish Cakes   23
Salmon Frumenty   21
Salmon, Sunday Roast   52
Salmon Trout, Baked   67
Salmon, Cú Chulainn   24
Sauce, Boiled Mayonnaise   34
Sausage Rolls   38
Sausages, Stuffed   29
Savoury Pancakes   176
Scallion Champ   49
Scones Made With Cream   177
Seafood Crumble, Wild Atlantic   24
Seafood Salad, Old Dublin   35
Seed Cake with Almonds   82
Semolina Jelly   108
Semolina Pudding   93
Serving Summer Fruits   99
Shelled Hemp Soda Bread   175
Sherry   71
Sligo Slop   131
Sloe & Apple Jelly   146
Smoked Haddock & Cheese Savoury   42
Smoked Salmon Surprise, West Coast   53
Soft Irish Brown Soda Bread / Wheaten Bread   155
Sole, Fillet of, with Irish Dulse Seaweed   26
Sophia's Soda Bread   178
Spelt Bread   176
Spiced Beef   63
Sponge Cake   71
Stampy Bread – a type of Boxty   172
St. Patrick's Pudding   60
Steak, Gaelic   43
Steamed Scrap Bread Pudding   70
Stout Bread   173
Stout Stew   20
Strawberry & Gooseberry Jam   143
Strawberry Crush   125
Stuffing, Old-fashioned   40
Sultana Bran Soda Bread   165
Sultana Scones   157

Tapioca & Apple Pudding   94
Teabread   170
The Blarney Stone   134
The Irish Blackthorn   133
The Tipperary Cocktail   135
Toffee Sauce   101
Tomato Bread   174
Tomato Sauce   46
Tory Island Cabbage   60
Treacle Bread   163
Treacle Fadge Farls   163
Trout grilled over an open fire   18
Trout, Skellig Islands   26
Tuesday's Pudding / Steamed Scrap Bread Pudding   70
Turnip au Gratin   65

Ulster Fry Paddy's Pizza   167
Urney Pudding   66

Veal Stuffing   54
Veal, Stewed Stuffed Shoulder of Irish Rosé Veal   54
Vegetable Marrow Bake   23
Vine Tomatoes stuffed with Irish Smoked Salmon   37
Vinegar Pastry   62
Vintage Irish Cider Fruit Cup Recipe   132

Wheaten Bread   154, 162
Wheaten Fadge   57
Wheaten Scones, County Tyrone   158
Whiskey Honey   139
Whiskey Sauce for Puddings   107
Whiskey Tea Bread   170

Yogurt & Banana Bread   175
Yogurt Cake, Gluten Free   80
Yogurt Scones   157

Afternoon Tea Menu

Coconut Scones (p 160)
Bramley Apple Scones (p 172)
Lemon & Rose Curd (p 147)
Blackcurrant Jam (p 146)
Rose Petal Jelly (p 148)
Whipped Cream

~

Selection of Irish Cheeses
Spelt Bread (p 176)

~

Irish Coffee Dessert Cake (p 109)
Irish Plate Apple Tart - thin pastry (77)

St Valentine's Day Menu

Cú Chulainn Salmon (p 24)
Fresh Market Vegetables
Prátaí Inis Ceithleann (p 39)

~

Honeycomb Cheesecake (p 89)

~

Emerald Isle Cocktail (p133)

St. Patrick's Day Party Menu

Stuffed Sausages (p 29)
Pancakes Colleen (p 18)
Belfast Chip Shop Pasties (p 37)

~

Brown Stew (p 19)
Creamy Colcannon Mash (p 20)

Irish Mixed Grill (p 18)

Lentil Irish Stew (p 49)

Irish Hotch Potch (p 41)

St. Patrick's Day Party Menu

Bride's Slices (p 116)
Fifteens (p114)
Gur Cake (p 122)
Granny's Favourite Traybake (p120)

~

Mint Choc Bubble Bar Cheesecake (p 91)
St. Patrick's Pudding (p 60)

~

Porter Cake (p 75)

~

Vintage Irish Cider Fruit Cup (p 132)
Misty Irish Cocktail (p 138)
Irish Shamrock (p 140)
Irish Shillelagh (p 135)
Irish Tea (p 137)

Saturday Evening Dining In Menu

Gaelic Steak (p 48)
Minted Peas (p 51)
Scallion Champ (p 49)

~

Bramley Apple Meringue Pudding (p 92)
Whipped Cream

Sunday Night Supper Menu

Filled Savoury Pancakes (p 176)

Little Pheasant Creams (p 45)

~

Apple Tart - deep pastry (p 78)

Lemon Coconut Slices (p 117)

~

Non-Alcoholic Irish Coffee (p 130)

Camp Fire Supper Menu

Buttermilk Point Picnic Loaf & Soft Cream Cheese
(p 168)

Freshly Caught Trout Grilled Over The Camp Fire
(p 18)

Dublin Rarebit (p28)

~

Bramley Apple Gingerbread (p 82)

~

Redcurrant Fudge (p 123)

Children's Birthday Party Menu

Homemade Sausage Rolls (p 38)
Paddy's Pizzas (p 166) - topped with ham & pineapple
pepperoni / four cheeses

~

Belfast Florence Cake, with candles (p 73)

~

Apple Hedgehogs (p 58)
Pineapple Creams (p 84)
Marshmallow Crispy Squares (p 114)
Donkey Lugs (p 181)

Notes

Notes

14902600R00120

Printed in Great Britain
by Amazon.co.uk, Ltd.,
Marston Gate.